BRADFORD

history & guide

BRADFORD

history & guide

Bob Duckett and John Waddington-Feather

TEMPUS

frontispiece General view of Bradford from Cliff Quarry, showing the saucer-shaped nature of Bradford and the stone quarry in the foreground. *Illustrated London News*, 20 September 1823. (Bradford Libraries)

First published 2005

Tempus Publishing Limited
The Mill, Brimscombe Port,
Stroud, Gloucestershire, GL5 2QG
www.tempus-publishing.com

© Bob Duckett and John Waddington-Feather, 2005

The right of Bob Duckett and John Waddington-Feather to be identified as the Authors of this work has been asserted in accordance with the Copyrights, Designs and Patents Act 1988.

British Library Cataloguing in Publication Data.
A catalogue record for this book is available from the British Library.

ISBN 0 7524 3702 X

Typesetting and origination by Tempus Publishing Limited
Printed in Great Britain

Contents

Preface and Acknowledgements

Having long voiced the view that what was needed was a popular history of Bradford, it proved impossible to back out of the corner I had driven myself into when asked to write one! In vain I protested that there were others more knowledgeable, more skilled and better qualified to write one. But, faced with a history or no history, I accepted the challenge.

I was helped in this decision by the generosity of John Waddington-Feather. In the late 1960s, John was commissioned to write a history of Bradford, to follow his history of Leeds that had been published earlier. He had got to 1850 when his publisher went out of business. John's typescript gathered dust until 1997. Then he gave it to me, saying, 'Use the typescript how you will'. So when that nice man from Tempus put me on the spot, I knew that part of the book had already been written! Forty years on and a different publisher, I had to modify and shorten John's text, but much remains. It is for this reason that his name appears on the title page. Thanks, John, I hope you approve!

The sources used to write this book are too numerous to identify and list, although we have noted any items quoted. Bradford has been fortunate in its historians, past and present. John James, William Scruton and William Cudworth of the older generation are three that come to mind. As I roam the streets of Bradford, I wish someone would emulate these pioneers and update their work. Of the moderns I wish to acknowledge, in particular, the work of Horace Hird, Joe Fieldhouse, George Sheeran, Gary Firth, David James and Clem Richardson.

I had the privilege of seeing Clem's book *Greater Bradford* through the press and I recall walking up Great Horton Road one sunny day to take him the proofs for his approval. Having just finished going through them myself, my head was stuffed full of Bradford knowledge. Though I was familiar enough with that long walk up Great Horton Road, this particular afternoon I was seeing the familiar with new eyes. Instead of the Asian restaurant, I was seeing an Irish tenement; instead of a cash-and-carry, I was seeing a coal staithe; and instead of a traffic-choked A647, I was seeing green fields with fleeces drying on the walls. It was an exciting experience. I was seeing a new Bradford, several Bradfords, all from years ago. If John and I can convey only part of this excitement, then we will have been successful.

I would like to acknowledge the assistance given me by the staff of Bradford's Museums Service, to Peter Walker for scanning John's yellowing typescript, and to Carol Greenwood and the staff of the Local Studies Library in Bradford. Without the museum and library staff there would be very little of Bradford's history left. Bless you all. May the Past ever be your Future!

Most importantly, I thank my wife, Pam. Her forbearance of my unsociability as I lived in the past instead of the present is deeply appreciated.

In conclusion, I quote from *It's a Mean Old Scene*, that hard-hitting and exciting history of post-1974 Bradford written by another inspirational chronicler of the Bradford scene, Jim Greenhalf. As I despair of trying to write the perfect history and pick my way, camera in hand, across the seemingly endless building site that is Bradford today, Jim provides the challenging riposte to the gloom felt by Bradford-born author J.B. Priestley, when he wrote: 'Bradford is a good place for discouragement'. Writes Jim:

> Whatever year it is when you read this book the Bradford that you behold will not be the city it was when you were born, nor the city that you remember as you grew up. Thirty years hence Bradford will be marked by more changes. Change is dynamic. Cities that remain static die. Bradford is not going to die, but it is going to change.

I'm sure Jim, like myself and countless others, have stood by Ian Judd's marvellous statue of 'JB' outside the National Museum of Photography, Film and Television, ears deafened by coach loads of excited children rushing around this 'visitor attraction' and the traffic tearing along the dual carriageway in front, and, following the Grand Old Man's gaze at the view across to the leafy/gothic cityscape ahead, have felt proud of Bradford; proud *to be* Bradford; even for us 'furriners'. I don't know why we feel proud. 'We're different here, mate', said one Asian lad to me the other day. Let's just leave it at that. To be a Bradfordian is to be different, defiant even; proudly defiant. Despite our problems, and we have many problems, ours is a vibrant place. In 1535 an earlier chronicler, John Leland, characterised Bradford as: 'A praty quik [lively] market toune'. It still is. And may it ever be so!

Note: photographs not by or from author's own collection are credited in captions.

Bob Duckett
Bradford, June 2005

chapter one

Bradford Dale: The Place

The name Bradford Dale is not much used today, which is unfortunate, because it reminds us that Bradford is a Pennine dale, and once had the scenic qualities that now attract countless visitors to the Yorkshire Dales each year.

(C. Richardson, *A Geography of Bradford*)

Bradford is one of the many towns that make up the West Yorkshire conurbation. Administratively, West Yorkshire is made up of the five Metropolitan Districts that were created under the Local Government Act which came into force in 1974. These five are Bradford, Calderdale, Kiklees, Leeds and Wakefield. This Act brought together a much larger number of authorities which had previously been independent – in the case of Bradford these were the city of Bradford itself, Ilkley, Bingley, Shipley and Keighley – or which had been part of the West Riding County Council, such as Baildon and Queensbury. Even today, over thirty years on, people have difficulty in understanding the nature of these 'metropolitan' areas and identify more with the older townships and neighbourhoods that preceded them. There are many reasons for this but one of them is geography. We identify with the physical region in which we live or work. This in turn relates to the history of the area and has little to do with the political and administrative logic that underlay the changes of 1974, which was based largely on balancing population figures. Few of us now remember that the 1974 Act also created the Metropolitan County Councils of West and South Yorkshire; these lasted a mere twelve years and survive only in a few services such as archives, archaeology and trading standards services. The point here is that 'our' locality is that which we can easily see and move around in and call 'home'.

The arbitrary nature of the 1974 Act can be seen in some of the disputes that took place prior to the Act about borders and 'who belongs to whom' – disputes that rumble on still. The ongoing creation of parish and local councils is testimony to the need for a 'local' voice. This is not to decry the administrative need for large metropolitan areas for a number of purposes, but in considering the history of a place it makes sense to relate it to the physical characteristics that 'define' a place. In this case we are 'defining' Bradford as the valley of the

Bradford Beck and its tributaries that flow north into the River Aire at Shipley: that saucer-shaped depression bounded by the Pennine foothills to the west, the southern hinterland that divides the catchment areas of the Aire and Calder rivers, and the higher ground to the east. Broadly speaking, this is the pre-1974 City of Bradford.

Geology

So much in the history of peoples living in an area stems from the geology of that area, and from other influences such as the climate which are complementary to geological study. Thus the carboniferous rocks that lie under the modern Bradford have imposed a character on the natural and man-made landscape. Examples are the near-flat surfaces of the bordering plateau, the valley 'benches', the steep hills, and the local sandstone of its buildings. Importantly, the rapid nineteenth-century growth of the city was based in the variety of coals, ironstones and other useful minerals present in the local rocks.

The northern edge of the Yorkshire coalfield runs across from Denholme by Shipley and Kirkstall to the north of Leeds, with Baildon Moor and Rawdon as outliers. The nearest points to Bradford where coal was first worked were Baildon Moor (where Tudor bell-workings were once thought to be the site of Iron Age dwellings) and Low Moor, where local coal was used for the purpose of smelting the iron-ore. Extensive faulting occurred, bringing to the surface a variety of rocks. There are bands of coal in the south and west of the Dale, and other rocks are shales, mudstones and sandstone, of which Gaisby Rock is a useful building stone quarried along the western side of the valley. Related to the coal seams are outcrops of ironstones and fireclay. Elland Flags sandstone, which used to be extensively quarried at Idle and other places around Bradford, makes up much of the higher ground around the city. It forms good building stone where it is found in bulk and the thinner flags are used as roofing slates, so characteristic a feature of farmhouses still in the Bradford and south Craven area.

Millstone Grit was quarried at places like Baildon Green, Horsforth and Yeadon. Many of the older houses in Bradford are built from this stone, which darkens in colour with weathering and gives the dry-stone walls their traditionally dark grey colouring as they vein the hillsides of the moorland farms on the Pennine Hills. It is the Millstone Grit escarpments which give the surrounding dales, moorland and countryside some of their more spectacular sights, as at Brimham Rocks, Addingham and Ilkley Moors, and the Otley Chevin. It is the same grit which, when broken down, provides the acid soil on which heather and peat flourish and, in the deep clefts formed by glacial movement, such as at Shipley Glen, makes possible a soil on which woodlands can grow.

The deep geological structure of Bradford, therefore, plays an important part in the shaping of the natural and urban environment where the people of Bradford live.

It was during the Great Ice Age that much of the natural landscape in and around Bradford was formed. Around 600,000 years ago a great climate change took place in the Northern Hemisphere. An ice-sheet spread gradually southwards over the Baltic and Scandinavia and eventually reached northern Britain, much of which developed local snow and ice-caps. The Vale of York was a huge glacier with fingers of ice reaching up the tributary dales, spreading over the intervening hills at times to link with adjoining dales and valleys.

The state of the ice-locked country was not permanent. Between 600,000 BC and 10,000 BC there were periods when the ice melted, to lesser or greater degrees, for several thousand years. As the ice melted, wholly or partially, during these Inter-Glacial periods, the ice-streams scoured the land, removing accumulated rock debris and soil, smoothing valley sides and hills, sometimes tearing out subsidiary ghylls or glens which coped with the melting waters from the hilltops, feeding these great ice-streams when the ice gradually melted. When it did melt, the ice deposited in the lowlands, and at intervals down the valleys, some of the material it had removed from the hills. This 'drift' material is to be found today in the boulder clay and moraines upon which Bradford is built.

Anyone who is an enthusiastic gardener in Bradford will have encountered boulder clay at some time or another. A look at any of the excavations for new buildings will also reveal evidence of it. The moraines are barrier-like ridges of boulders, gravel and clay across a valley floor. Most of the moraines were formed in the latter part of the Ice Age, when the ice was melting and the glaciers were withdrawing. This withdrawal was not constant, but when the 'front' of a glacier remained at the same position for a long time, the rock debris and boulders being melted out behind it were swept down the valley and deposited at the 'front' to form a kind of barrier. Sometimes when the glaciers retreated very rapidly, these moraines dammed up the melted ice behind them to form huge lakes, so that the Dales would look like a kind of Lake District. These lakes lasted, sometimes well into historic times, until they were either filled in by gravel and silt, or a deep channel was cut through the moraine by the emerging streams that are now the rivers of the different Dales valleys. The moraines now stand out as ridges high above the valley floor and in between them are low-lying flats that usually flood in winter. Near Bradford, moraines cross the Aire Valley floor at Apperley, Nab Wood, Bingley and Utley, near Keighley.

Many smaller lakes were trapped by the ice in tributary valleys and the basin in which Bradford is built was one such lake. As the ice melted, waters coming from 'Lake Worth' and draining across Oxenhope Moor overflowed at Bell Dean, near Thornton, coursed round by Close Top Farm, Great Horton and, by a great channel at Wibsey Bank Foot, they escaped from the Aire Valley into the ice-free country of the Spen Valley and Calderdale.

The lakes formed by the melting ice persisted long after the Ice Age had finished and frequently contain archaeological evidence of the types of animal living in these regions about the time man came. A dug-out canoe from the site of Giggleswick Tarn shows that these lakes persisted well after man's arrival on the scene.

In Bradford in 1920, cores of the horns of the aurochs, a prehistoric ox of massive size that lived from about 4,000 to 2,000 years ago, were found in the cellars of Russell Buildings, Leeds Road, during excavations there. In January 1963, similar horn-cores were unearthed in Forster Square during the excavations for the foundations of the new buildings erected on the site.

Animal bones found in Yorkshire pre-dating the great Ice Age give some indication of the tropical climate that existed then. Hippopotami bones were found in the nineteenth century at Armley, Leeds, when the foundations for the gaol were being dug, and bones of hyenas, prehistoric elephants and rhinoceroses were found in the Victoria Cave at Settle. Other bones of typically tropical creatures were also quarried from limestone quarries at Lothersdale, near Skipton, and the most prolific pre-glacial finds to date were made in another former hyena den at Kirkdale, near Pickering in the East Riding.

After about 10,000 BC the ice-caps began to melt and Paleolithic (Early Stone Age) man, who had long been living south of the ice-line, began to move north. Upper Paleolithic remains of man were found in the South Pennines in the Cresswell Caves of Derbyshire, and also flint finds were made at Windy Hill, twelve miles from Huddersfield, below a deep layer of peat. These remains show that man lived on the southern boundaries of Yorkshire in early post-glacial times, in what must have been sub-arctic conditions which lasted till about 7,500 BC.

Gradually the weather improved and the climate around Bradford entered what is known as the Boreal climate period. It was dry with hot summers and cold winters and lasted from about 7,500 to 5,500 BC. Bradford at this time would have been a marshy lake in the basin on which it stands. The bleak landscape of the post-glacial phase underwent a slow change, very slow in the areas higher up the slopes because the soil there, except for the more fertile areas of drift soil such as on the moraines, would be sandy and infertile. The heights above Bradford about 8,500 years ago would be open sandy wastes broken by occasional birch and pine trees. Lower down the slopes, woods of oak, birch and alder would be growing thicker and creeping higher up the hillsides as the climate underwent yet another change, from 5,500 to about 3,000 BC, and became what is known as the Atlantic Period.

The weather of the Atlantic Period was warm and wet, making conditions better for tree growth. The woods became denser and covered the high ground that is the cotton-grass and heather moors today. Probably because of the increasing rainfall, changes slowly took place in the soil on which these upland forests were growing, changes that eventually turned the soil acidic and killed off the forests that covered the tops of the Pennine Hills. The salts which the Ice Age glaciers had brought down and covered the 'acidic' Millstone Grit rocks, salts which were essential for the growth of trees, were leached out of the upper layers of soil and left it poor in nutriment. Soluble iron compounds in the soil, moreover, with the action of alternately wet and dry periods, became insoluble iron oxides and an impermeable layer of oxides was formed which retained water and prevented drainage. The acid condition of the soil above this impermeable layer, called podsol, killed off bacteria and insects which help the decay of vegetable matter, so necessary for soil nutrition, and only plants such as cotton-grass were able to survive. The trees succumbed, bogs and marshland developed and through the centuries layer upon layer of peat – degenerating cotton-grass moss – were formed above the dead woodlands. The moors of the Pennines as we know them now had come into being.

Topgraphy

In modern times the built-up parts of Bradford have spread over the valley slopes to the flat-topped divide which separated the main drainage basins and spread southwards into the catchment area of the River Calder and northwards into the Airedale, but the main part of the town lies within Bradford Dale.

Bradford Dale is like a huge natural amphitheatre, almost completely enclosed by high land. Wherever you stand in Bradford Dale – from Undercliffe Cemetery, travelling down the Leeds Road, from Bowling Park, Wibsey, Clayton or Heaton – it is possible to see most of the town with the sweep of the eye. The views are spectacular. It is the nature of this valley that gave a sense of identity to its inhabitants, and still does, despite the administrative change made in 1974. It is why we define Bradford and Bradford Dale in this book.

Climate

With a height difference of 900 feet between the heights of Clayton and the low areas of the city centre, there can be a wide variation in rainfall and temperature. Heaton Reservoir has an annual rainfall of 34.15 inches (867 mm)

below left Downhill all the way: a view taken from near the frontispiece picture. Kings Road, Bolton Woods.

below right The Bradford Beck today. The river that played such a great part in the history of Bradford is almost totally buried until it reaches Shipley! Here it passes under Shipley station.

and Lister Park an annual mean temperature of 47.9°F (8.8°C) and 1,242 hours of sunshine. For comparison, York has 24.7 inches of rain, a 49.3°F (9.6°C) mean temperature and 1,304 hours of sunshine. With the greater altitude causing greater rainfall and reduced sunshine and temperature, Bradford Dale is not well suited to agriculture. It does, however, lie in the rain shadow of the Pennines and benefits from the warming effect of the prevailing westerly winds, and is hence better-off than the neighbouring lands in Lancashire. The winds are generally light, and although the pall of smoke that used to hang over the city for weeks on end has been eliminated by Clean Air legislation, pollution haze does still feature on occasions.

Bradford has a growing season of about seven months in the lower Dale and about six months above 750 feet, though since there is a risk of frosts through to May and from September, the season is sometimes shorter. The soils are naturally acidic due to a high silica content and the leaching effect of high rainfall. In addition, the area has a high percentage of slopes in excess of 1 in 10 which produces a fast run-off. Conversely, the deeper soils in the valley bottoms retain water and are slow to warm. Although of minor importance today, farming was the major activity for most of Bradford's history, and even now large parts of Bradford Dale can be classed as farmland.

Even today, much of Bradford Dale is rural. Park Hill Farm, Thackley.

chapter two

Early Bradford Man

The Stone Age

The Mesolithic Age (Middle Stone Age, 7,000-3,000 BC) spanned the cold, dry Boreal and the mild, damp Atlantic Periods of climate change. No flints of Mesolithic man so far have been found in the actual Bradford area, though there were Mesolithic sites at Oxenhope Moor and Baildon Moor, so Middle Stone Age man was living in the vicinity. He may, however, have stayed in this part of Yorkshire only very temporarily, possibly on hunting expeditions in pursuit of migrating herds. With the onset of harsh winters, in all probability the Mesolithic hunters would have retraced their steps back to warmer areas in the south of England or the Continent. The finds which have been made near Bradford are usually found over 1,000 feet.

Finds of later Neolithic (New Stone Age) man have been made in and near Bradford. Two factors may have encouraged settlement in the Bradford region during the Neolithic Age (3,000-1,600 BC). The weather was warmer and Neolithic man was a farmer as opposed to a hunter. He had learnt the art of agriculture and had developed stone axes which could fell trees and so clear land. There are many examples of these stone axes found in Bradford and quite a few arrowheads and a cinery urn have also been discovered. These Neolithic farmers left traces of their settlement at such places as Ravenscliffe, Eccleshill, Heaton, Wibsey and Baildon, at all of which places leaf-shaped arrowheads have been found. Stone and flint axeheads have also been dug up at Lidget Green, Bolton Woods, Clayton and Five Lane Ends, Idle.

The Bronze Age

The Neolithic Age is terminated by the Early Bronze Age (1,650-1,300 BC). The age dates are arbitrary and the probability is that bronze and stone implements would be used at the same time as each other. The new people who came into the Bradford area would drift in gradually, living side by side with the earlier inhabitants until the earlier ones were assimilated and their culture superseded.

The Early Bronze Age people are called the Beaker folk, on account of the pottery they used. They were different in ethnic type from the Neolithic folk, for they were taller and had rounder heads, contrasting with the long-headed Neolithic people who were rarely more than five feet in height. They were also nomadic and pastoral as opposed to the settlers of the earlier age. They probably carried their food in the beakers for which they are renowned, invading Yorkshire and Eastern England directly from the Rhinelands. Their beakers also held fermenting liquor, for they had discovered the methods – and delights – of making alcoholic drink.

Although the people of this era knew the use of bronze, they still often used flint and stone in their implements, but unlike the leaf-shaped arrowheads of the Neolithic people, the Beaker folk used barbed and tanged arrowheads of flint. Examples of these arrowheads have been found on Baildon Moor, West Bowling, Thornton and Eccleshill; an axe-hammer was also found in a quarry at Eccleshill.

The most significant finds of Early Bronze Age man have been the cup and ring markings on boulders around Bradford. Just what the use and meaning of these markings were is not clear. It is thought they were of religious significance for nearly all of them are on elevated, south-facing sites which receive the sun all day. Those in the Bradford area are at Northcliffe Woods, Baildon Moor and Hirst Wood. It is interesting to note that they are the earliest stone carvings discovered on rock surfaces in the North of Britain till nearly 2,000 years later in the Christian era. The majority are found only in the north of England and south Scotland in Britain and the religious culture, if they have a religious meaning, must have been pretty intense in the Bradford region if the number and quality of finds are any criterion.

Soon after the Beaker folk had settled in Yorkshire the practice was to deposit food-vessels instead of beakers with the dead. This change of custom led to the gradual disuse of the beaker and the development of cinerary urn usage with cremation instead of burial of the dead. The food-vessels are much more numerous than beakers, and are more widely distributed, indicating a growing population.

The colonies of Early Bronze Age man living in the Bradford area may have grown as a result of the Ireland/Scandinavia trade route of Bronze Age times passing just north of Bradford. Ireland was a chief source of copper, gold and tin in prehistoric days. Trade routes in these commodities would traverse Northern England from the West Coast, via the Aire Gap and the moorlands between Airedale and Wharfedale, on to the Yorkshire Wolds, and then to the East Coast. From there they could cross the North Sea by primitive watercraft.

The Middle Bronze Age was the final outcome of the mingling of cultures and races that had been going on for over 300 years. Its most noticeable feature was the cremating of the dead and their ashes being interred in hand-made urns, called cinerary urns. From this practice we call them the Urn Folk. The urns were usually placed in round barrows (mounds of earth) ranging from 18 to 80 feet in diameter and from 2 to 12 feet in height. Finds around Bradford from the Middle Bronze Age include a flanged bronze axe found at Bolton, socketed axes from Baildon Moor and Apperley Bridge, and food vessels from Baildon Moor. Sometimes the Urn folk buried their dead within circles of earth and stone. Several of the stone circles on the moors around Bradford may well have been originally Urn folk burial sites, with the actual burial places long since plundered and gone. The Grubstones on Burley Moor and the Twelve Apostles between Bingley and Ilkley may well have indicated these burial sites.

One interesting feature is the prevalence of standing stones which are sometimes seen in the fields around Bradford. The upright stone cult reached Yorkshire from the Mediterranean, where the Egyptians made it a fine art with their obelisks. Metal traders and migrants slowly brought the cult northwards, and it was eventually adopted by the Early Bronze Age invaders and developed to its height during the Middle Bronze Age. Possibly the upright stones were of phallic significance, built to induce fertility into the settlement and its stock near which they stood. Many of these stones may have been incorporated as stoop stones in modern field walls, especially on the moors, and the various patterns of wall-capping, such as buck and doe wall-capping, may all be survivals of the lively religious practices of the Bronze Age folk.

The Late Bronze Age extended in England from about 1200 BC to 500 BC, although, like the previous ages, there was no definite period in time when the Bronze Age implements and its culture ceased to be used and Iron Age ones taken up.

There are several Late Bronze Age burial mounds on Baildon Moor. Late Bronze Age cinerary urns were found at Lower Headley, Thornton, in 1880, and cinerary urns and an incense cup were found at Chellow Heights in 1921. Axes have also been discovered at Eldwick and Baildon.

The Iron Age

Throughout prehistoric times, it would appear that the North, and especially the West Riding, was a backwater for the development of the various cultures of the peoples invading Britain. There are few of the elaborate prehistoric settlements and sophisticated artefacts which are a feature of the South of England and, to some extent, the East Riding, during the Bronze Age. The same lack of finds of sophisticated manufactures and goods during the Early Iron Age indicates a primitive iron culture in the Bradford area right through this period to the Roman occupation. Compared with the finds around York and in the South of England, the materials discovered in the same period in and around Bradford are very primitive.

By 500 BC the South of England was rich in settled hamlets and farmsteads, whereas in the North many of the Urn folk were still leading semi-nomadic lives, probably because the weather was inclement and pasturage poor on the

Pennine slopes. The development of manufacturing in, and trade of, bronze implements had led to a prosperous civilization which had grown throughout Western Europe. There was better farming and much better standards of living with more comfortable homesteads, better food and better clothes. The coming of the Iron Age brought further material development, though implements such as cooking utensils are remarkably ugly in this Early Iron Age period compared with the ornate and beautiful craftsmanship of the preceding Bronze Age. Iron at first was not very much superior to bronze, but it was infinitely more plentiful and easy to come by as a natural ore. Once the smelting techniques of iron had been mastered, it could be produced in much greater quantity and much more cheaply than bronze.

Around 500 BC the worsening of the climate began to have a serious effect on the farming tribes of northern Europe. Longer, harsher winters meant that crops could not be sown in time for them to ripen and consequently the lack of a harvest meant that more northerly peoples had not sufficient food to see them through the winter. Threatened with famine they migrated south and the pressure of these migrants, and an already universal growth in population, pushed the Celts of central Europe westwards. They, in turn, migrated to Britain and brought with them a late version of the iron culture which marks the beginning of the first real British Iron Age around 500 BC, although the occasional use of iron implements had been known earlier. The Celts did not come all together. There were a series of invasions extending from 500 BC right down to about 75 BC with each successive wave of Celtic immigrants tending to push earlier groups more and more westwards.

Iron Age farm settlements and forts have been found in some quantities around Bradford. An Iron Age farm would cultivate about 15 acres of arable land, of which 5 acres only would be sown in any one year. Land around Bradford would be difficult to settle owing to poor weather and thick, dense woodland and marsh in the valley bottoms. Poor soil would preclude any arable farming on a large scale, and the Iron Age farmer in the Bradford area doubtless would have to supplement his food by such game as he could hunt in the neighbouring woodlands.

Farming equipment in this Early Iron Age period would comprise a two-ox plough (in the more fertile areas), iron sickles and querns for grinding flour by rubbing a small stone on a larger one. Perhaps very primitive methods of ploughing, such as hand-ploughing, were still in use around Bradford even as late as 500 BC, for no finds that might have been iron-shod ploughs have turned up in the area, although many querns have been found. Beehive querns have been found at Bingley, Bracken Hall (Baildon) and Girlington, and more may be lurking unidentified as rockery ornaments in gardens around Bradford. Iron Age mortars have been found at Clayton and Cottingley, and an iron sickle was discovered in 1964 at Bracken Hall Green.

All these finds indicate smallish but extensive settlements around Bradford; settlements relatively primitive in culture compared with the more complex social structures of the same period in other parts of Yorkshire and England.

There is nothing, for example, on the same scale as the large Iron Age fort at Aldmondbury near Huddersfield, or the Iron Age towns at Aldborough, Driffield and Scarborough.

The climate of the Iron Age was colder and wetter than at present and the Iron Age farmer in these Pennine areas lived in impoverished conditions. Some idea of the small size of their farmsteads can be gauged from the walling and enclosures discovered at Crosley Wood, Gilstead, which only cover about 5 acres all told. The amount of Romano-British pottery found on this site also indicates a very small settlement.

A second important Celtic Iron Age invasion about 300 BC was made by bands of warriors which caused panic among the population of Britain. They came from La Tene, around Lake Constance, and brought new skilful methods of working iron. They had been influenced very much by the Greek civilisation in their culture, both artistically and militarily, and were skilful in the use of chariot-fighting.

The native Celts and Bronze Age folk hastily began to throw up earthworks to protect themselves against this new wave of invaders. They dug ditches round their homesteads and made formidable hill-forts on the crests of the hills around their settlements. The hill fort on the top of Ingleborough may have been started in this way, though it was probably used later as successive waves of other invaders continued to move into the West Riding.

The La Tene people enslaved the earlier Hallstatt Celts and established a Celtic aristocracy in Yorkshire. One band of La Tene invaders settled in the Craven area and a beautiful necklace was found at Embsay which is associated with them. The swastika rock-carving at Ilkley is also thought to have been made by them. No finds, however, have been made in the immediate Bradford vicinity, and the Celts living around the Bradford area may well have been an isolated pocket of people, no doubt influenced from time to time by surrounding groups of more highly civilised settlers and invaders, such as the inhabitants of the Roman fort at Ilkley, but by and large living out their own lives in rather backward conditions.

By about 100 BC the invaders of the West Riding had become sufficiently intermingled and settled to emerge as a Celtic group we call the Brigantes. The chief town of the Brigantian people was at Aldborough, given the Latin name of Isurium in Romano-British times. They were a separate group of Celts from the East Riding settlers who were called the Parisii, who migrated from northern France and later gave their name to the present capital of France. In a similar way the Brigantes probably came from around Lake Constance, on the Austro-Swiss borders, the main town of which is still called Brigenz.

The Brigantes were notable warrior people who gave the Romans a deal of trouble when they in turn conquered the area around Bradford. In primitive Brigantian warrior society head-hunting and the display of heads was an important religious feature. The human head was probably thought to be the seat of physical as well as mental prowess, so that the lopping off of enemy heads and displaying them in one's household transferred extra power to the victor in primitive societies. Later, the powers of the real human head were transferred to replicas of it. Stone heads, therefore, were sculptured, and the oldest stone heads discovered in the Bradford area date from the early Celtic period. This particular custom of head sculpture has gone on continuously in Craven from that period to the present and the Museum Service has a very good collection of stone heads from the Celtic period onwards. Odd stone heads still turn up in walls and gardens around Bradford, but although not all of them belong to the Celtic period, it is interesting to note how this tradition has been maintained throughout West Yorkshire, when it has died out in all other parts of Britain.

Though the Romans invaded the South of England in 55 BC under Julius Caesar, they made no further advance upcountry till AD 43. During the intervening century, however, Roman traders ventured further north, and contacted the Brigantian tribes through trade channels. The Brigantes had their own coinage, but the Judean coin of Herod Agrippa (AD 37-44) found on Gilstead Moor in 1947 may have been brought to Yorkshire during this period. The bulk of Roman coins in the Bradford area postdate the AD 43 Roman campaign.

The Celtic Brigantian queen of the Bradford area during this second Roman 'push' north was Queen Cartimandua, a pro-Roman queen who married an anti-Roman husband, Venutius, who later established a resistance movement against the invading Romans and left his queen. Venutius established his guerrilla headquarters in the hill fort of Ingleborough and the anti-Roman faction of West Yorkshire rallied round him there. (Cartimandua, incidentally, issued her own coinage and in 1893 some of her coins were discovered at Honley, near Huddersfield. Her betrayal of Caractacus to the Romans in AD 51 may well have precipitated the break with her husband.)

Brigantian tribesmen from the Bradford region would possibly have helped Venutius in his guerrilla attacks upon the Roman army trying to subdue Yorkshire. In AD 69 he started to prepare a vast hill fort at Stanwick, near Richmond, and summoned the aid of Brigantes from a wide area, even from Scotland, to help him meet the Roman attack he knew was inevitable.

The Romans had possibly met local South Craven resistance from the defenders of such earthworks as that on Cullingworth Moor, Castle Stead Ring. Originally this earthwork had a rampart 6 feet high, and a ditch 4 feet deep, but most of this has since been ploughed up. The whole site was about 2 acres in area, minute really in comparison with the guerrilla fort at Stanwick, which covered 850 acres and was surrounded by ramparts at times 20 feet high.

The Romans under Petilius attacked Stanwick before the fortifications were complete and Venutius was defeated. The Brigantes retreated back to such places as the Bradford settlement. A great expansion of Iron Age dwellings and field systems began after Venutius's defeat in AD 74 and the Romans also began lead-mining in the Dales on a very commercial scale. (The Brigantes continued to harass the Romans long after their defeat at Stanwick, though, and revolted again very violently nearly 200 years later.)

After the defeat of Venutius, the Roman governor, Petilius, set up an administrative centre over West Yorkshire at Isurium (Aldborough, near Boroughbridge). A fort was also built later at Olicanum (Ilkley) from which the Roman legions would enforce their authority on the Brigantes living in the hills around Bradford. A spreading road network, often going near to Celtic settlements, brought the authority of Rome much nearer to the Brigantes.

The Romano-British Period (AD 110-500)

Though the Brigantian settlements around Bradford appeared to remain relatively unaffected by Roman occupation of the area, there are many signs of Roman control and exploitation. Coin-finds are the principal source of evidence, but other archaeological remains, such as roads and iron workings, indicate Roman interest in this region.

Roman influence was not very great in Bradford itself as there are only one or two place names directly concerned with Roman occupation, but there are many more Celtic place names that have come down to us. The name of the River Aire comes from a Celtic word, *isara*, which meant 'a strong river'. The Wharfe, too, is closely connected with a Celtic goddess, Verbeia, whose name is found on a Roman inscription at Ilkley. Baildon is thought to have originated from a Celtic name, and Pennithorne Lane there, in the first element of the word, Penn, may have associations with the Celtic word *pen*, meaning the top, or summit of a hill. Penny Hill at Clayton may come from the same source. We find this element again in the place names Pennine and Penyghent. Eccleshill is a place name probably coined in late Romano-British times when the Brigantes living in the area had become Christianised and a church had been erected on the site. The element 'Eccles' in a place name very often referred to a pre-English church. The 'Eccles' element, which was known and understood by the invading pagan Germanic tribes after about AD 500, may well have been retained by them to denote the sites of Christian Celtic churches. (Later, when the Germanic invaders themselves became Christians, they used the element 'church' or 'kirk', as in Kirkstall, to denote the sites of their own churches.)

The Chevin at Otley is another modern name existing from Celtic times, coming from an Old Welsh word, *kefyn*, which meant 'a ridge'. The Craven district of Yorkshire which comes right down to Bradford's boundaries is also a Celtic name. 'Craven' comes from *kramo* which means 'garlic'. (Anyone with a keen nose walking through local woods in summer can bear testimony to the favourable conditions that garlic plants still find in some areas of West Yorkshire.) The larger region of Elmet, which formed a Celtic kingdom of which Bradford was a part right into the seventh century, also comes from an Old Welsh tribal name 'Elfed'.

Unlike other Yorkshire towns and cities, Bradford has only one or two place names to indicate Roman activity in the vicinity. These place names are usually associated with long roads or lanes which are called 'Street'. Tong Street is

one such place name. The invading Angles, who came after the Roman troops
pulled out of Britain, had already several Latin words in their vocabulary from
the contacts they had with Roman civilisation long before they invaded Britain.
One of these words was *straet* from the Latin word *stratam* which meant a road,
and from which derives 'straight'. It was natural for the Angles then to give the
name 'straet' to any stretch of Roman road that existed in the vicinity of their
first settlements, and Tong Street may well have been built on the site of a former
Roman road, probably built to facilitate carriage of products to and from the
Roman iron workings at Bierley. Another more obvious example of this sort
of naming by the Angles in the vicinity of Bradford is the name of Street Lane
at East Morton. This lane, leading out of the village up to Ilkley Moor, if not
forming part of the original Roman road itself, certainly links up with the Roman
road from Manchester to Ilkley, where the Romans built a very strong fort as a
military centre to control the Brigantes in Craven.

From about AD 82 the Romans consolidated their position in the West Riding
under the Roman governor Julius Agricola. Under Cerialis the Roman frontier
had been pushed north as far as Chester in the west and York (Eboracum) in
the east. Agricola pushed the boundaries further north and also built the first
network of roads in the Bradford area, including the Manchester-Ilkley road
just referred to. A second major road the Romans built in this period was a
trans-Pennine road starting at Ribchester ('camp on the Ribble') and coming
through Elslack and Skipton, down the Aire Valley through Keighley (where a
bronze eagle from a Roman Standard was found) and finishing at Bierley. This
trans-Pennine road crossed the Manchester-Ilkley road at Keighley and would
have been an important link road in the Roman road network. The Ilkley road
continued on to York where the famous Ninth Legion was quartered.

The Roman army of occupation comprised two types of troops, legionaries
and auxiliaries. The legions were about 6,000 strong and were citizens of the
Empire. The auxiliaries worked in units of about 500 to 1,000 men and were
conscripted from recently conquered frontier tribes. The auxiliaries were used
as frontline soldiers and took the brunt of any fighting. The more experienced
Roman legionaries being kept in the rear to consolidate and strengthen the area
there. The auxiliaries were stationed at outpost forts, such as those at Ilkley
and Elslack, but the powerful legions were quartered in rear bases, much more
highly developed cities like that at York. The Brigantian tribes around Bradford
in all probability would supply some troops to garrison the Ilkley fort. It is just
as likely that other neighbouring tribes would follow Brigantian rebels like
Venutius, and later King Arviragus, in their revolts against the Roman army.

Roman coins have been found over a wide area of Bradford indicating that
although the Brigantian settlements in the region absorbed little Roman culture,
there was a great deal of Roman activity in the area, such as troop movements
and commercial transportation. Roman coin finds have been made throughout
the city; at Idle, Heaton, Frizinghall, Esholt and a little further afield at Shipley,
Baildon Moor, Cottingley, Gilstead Moor and Wrose. The dates of the coins

range from the Judean-Roman coin of Herod Agrippa I (AD 37-44) found on Gilstead Moor in 1947 to another, found at the same time and place, of Constantine II (AD 317-337).

Ilkley was the nearest known Roman occupied site to Bradford, although the Roman road eventually crossing the Pennines connects Bierley directly with another Roman fort at Elslack in upper Craven. The church at Ilkley is built over much of the Roman fort there, but an interesting collection of remains unearthed from it is housed in Ilkley's Manor House Museum.

There was a serious revolt supported by the tribes around Bradford under Arviragus in AD 115 and many of the forts, including that at Ilkley, were destroyed. The Romans hastily sent reinforcements from the Continent and the Ninth Legion at York was either almost wiped out or disgraced in battle, for it was replaced at York by the Sixth Legion. Probably after this revolt the resistance fighters retreated back into the Dales with the plunder they had taken from the Roman forts. The Victoria Caves and other limestone caves have yielded large collections of Roman ornaments, indicating that these caves may have been places of shelter and retreat from retaliating Roman troops.

Ilkley was rebuilt in stonework as a fort in AD 125 when Hadrian was the military commander of Britain. He drew up a new plan of administering and patrolling the North, which included building the famous wall from the Solway to the Tyne, and the partial withdrawal of his troops from Scotland. The defence of his wall drew some of his troops from the Pennines, but the Sixth Legion at York seems to have been sufficient for holding down the warlike tribes of Brigantia.

AD 150 to AD 250 was a time of relative peace and prosperity for the Romano-British population of the West Riding. The native Celts were beginning to adopt Roman customs more and more, especially in the regions neighbouring Roman military strong points such as York, and, to a lesser extent, Elslack and Ilkley. There is, however, little evidence of the Celtic population around Bradford being much affected by Roman influence. The inclement weather, high altitude and poor arable land would all discourage much intense settlement such as we find in other parts of the county and in the more fertile parts of Craven. The odd finds of Roman coins, however, do suggest contact was becoming increasingly frequent between the hill tribes of Bradford and the Roman patrol forces stationed in the forts.

Towards the end of the third century there was a breakdown of authority within Roman rule and many troops were withdrawn from border forts to fight on one side or another of the rival Roman factions. The Pennine Brigantes, never really subjugated or civilised by the Romans, took advantage of the Romans' internal struggle for power and revolted. The occupation of the forts at Ilkley and Elslack was discontinued and the villa at Gargrave was sacked and burned by the Brigantes from the western Dales. In Bradford, the thriving iron industry at Bierley came to an untimely end about the same time or shortly afterwards early in the fourth century. Coins found in the iron slag heaps there have been associated with Diocletian, Carausius, Constantius and Constantine (AD 287-

306) but nothing later. The unsettled conditions at the end of the third century are also reflected in further Romano-British finds from the cave systems of the upper Dales, around Settle and Kilnsey, which, according to coin finds, were again occupied from about AD 253 to AD 340.

In 296, Constantius Chlorus, Caesar of the Western Empire, came north and crushed the Brigantian revolt. The York garrison, which had suffered severely in the rebellion, was rebuilt, but there was no serious attempt to re-establish the fort at Ilkley. Chlorus died at York, where he was buried in AD 306, and his son, Constantine, the first Christian emperor, became emperor in his stead. Like his father, Constantine was a fine leader and at his death in AD 337 he was emperor of both the East and West Roman empires. It was during Constantine's rule as emperor that Christianity first came to Yorkshire, about, if not before, AD 314.

Seventy years after Constantine's death, Rome withdrew her troops from Britain, a land already badly ravaged by invasions from Picts, Irish and, more increasingly, Saxon pirates. Excavations in Yorkshire have revealed the brutal and chaotic state the Romano-British communities were in. Towns and villas were being sacked and burned, their occupants slaughtered and their corpses flung into wells and shallow graves. For more than a hundred years there was a chronic state of warfare among invaders and rival Celtic tribes until an organised and systematic invasion by the Germanic peoples, the Angles, Saxons and Jutes, opened up another phase of British history.

The Anglo-Norse Period (500-1066)

One of the surprising things about the Anglo-Norse period in the Bradford area is that although the Anglo-Norse invaders gave Bradford, and Yorkshire, the early forms of its characteristic dialects and nearly all its place names, fewer archaeological remains have been found belonging to this period than any other. The only definitely proved Anglian remains found in the vicinity of Bradford have been some beads on Baildon Moor. Why this should be so was probably because the Anglians had not penetrated very far west in their pre-Christian era. However, a pretty comprehensive picture of the region around Bradford can be drawn from a study of its place names, dialects and, to a lesser extent, from the entries in Domesday Book drawn up around 1080.

The Anglo-Saxons came first as raiding parties before the Romans pulled out of Britain. After the withdrawal of Roman troops, more Anglo-Saxon tribes entered the country. They were mainly Anglian tribes who settled the Bradford region, probably coming from North Germany and South Denmark. The Saxons tended to colonise the southern part of the country, which accounts for the widely different dialects spoken today in the North and South of England.

As the colonising Anglians moved westwards they encountered more difficult and less fertile land in the foothills of the Pennines. The great forest of Elmet spread from the Pennine hills far in the west and came down to link up with the woodlands of Nottinghamshire. The valley floors were wild swampy places and the hillsides covered with thick scrub which eventually gave way to bleak moorland. Not an inviting place for the majority of the Anglian farming settlers who probably left the colonising of the Pennine West Riding to smaller groups.

These smaller groups, if place names are anything to go by, tended to live peaceably side by side with the native Celtic peoples and eventually intermixed with them through marriage. The Anglian farmers seemed to be more advanced in clearing the thick wooded valley floors and draining them than the native Celts, whose settlements were generally found on the naturally drained parts of the hillsides and tops. Further evidence supporting the theory that the Anglians lived more peaceably alongside their Celtic neighbours in the Bradford region is their retention of Celtic place and river names rather than re-naming of them.

We can hazard a guess from the research done into place names what places within the city boundaries were first colonised by the Anglian settlers. We can also build up a picture of what the terrain looked like when these Germanic invaders first came. The many references to clearings in woods or the clearings in marshland present a very different picture of the Bradford of 1,400 years ago from the Bradford of today.

Place names that are tribal names, i.e. names of groups of people that have been transferred to places, probably indicate primary settlement. The place names ending in '-ing', or having it as a compound such as '-ingham' or '-ington', show where the Anglians first settled. 'Ingas' meant 'people of', or 'children of', so Manningham was 'homestead of Maegen's people'. Girlington was 'the village or settlement of Gyrla's folk'. Probably some closely related people from the borders of what are modern Germany and Holland came over and settled later amongst the Anglian colonists, for the name Frizinghall can mean 'the Frisian's nook of land'. Thornton was an enclosure made of thorns, a very necessary place when the area was still inhabited by bears and wolves, to say nothing of potentially hostile Celts and incoming tribes.

Other districts of Bradford where primary settlement took place and where the first Anglian pockets of colonists built their farmsteads would be spots like Bolton, coined from two Old English words *bothl* and *tun* and meaning 'an enclosure with buildings', i.e. a small village; Allerton, a farmstead among the alder trees; Clayton, a farmstead built on clay; Heaton, the high farmstead; Horton, a filthy farm; Bierley, a small dwelling place; Tyersal, Tir's nook of land.

Secondary settlements would take place some distance from the original farmstead or village. Once the Anglian coloniser had established his home farm he would then make further clearings in the surrounding brushwood or scrub and attempt cultivation of the higher ground. Place names with the elements '–hirst', '-ley', '-haw' and '-wood' in them today are derived from Old English (the language spoken by the Germanic settlers) and mean 'woods' or 'clearings in woods'. Later Germanic invaders, the Norsemen, who spoke a language closely related to Old English called Old Norse, also named their settlements from words meaning clearings in woods and some of these Old Norse elements are '-lund' and '-scar'.

There are many place names around Bradford ending in '-ley', such as Bingley, Shipley, Keighley, and it is interesting to note that these valley place names are located on or near the glacial moraines that stretched across the valley floor. The moraines would stand out as wooded ridges surrounded by marsh and, being naturally well drained, would be attractive places to establish a settlement, being relatively dry yet near good water supplies.

Outstanding natural features, of course, would be named by the Anglians. Where a place name is derived from a natural feature it indicates later settlement than those place names derived from personal or tribal names. Bradford itself falls into this category. It means 'the broad ford', the ford presumably being one which carried a wide track across Bradford Beck in the centre of the present town, which was then very swampy. Other Bradford district place names which show us what the area was like in Anglo-Norse times are: Bowling, a bowl-shaped hollow; Chellow, a hill or mound; Esholt, an ash wood; Idle, an empty, uncultivated place; Tong, a spit of land.

Once the Anglians had settled down, the gradual process began of developing a political identity. From being isolated settlements, the earliest sites around Bradford began to group together. 'Shires', that is shares of land, were allocated to various groups to administer and rule over. Bradford was first of all in the ancient Celtic kingdom of Elmete, then later it became part of Deira about AD 616, which in turn was part of the great Anglian kingdom of Northumbria.

Edwin, the king of Northumbria, was the first Anglian king to become a Christian when he married Ethelburga, daughter of the Saxon king of Kent, in AD 625. However, Edwin's conversion to Christianity brought him into conflict with Penda, the heathen king of Mercia, the kingdom of the Midlands. Penda invaded Northumbria with a strong army of veterans and killed Edwin at the Battle of Hatfield, near Doncaster in AD 633.

Penda set up a series of puppet rulers in Northumbria and possibly it was during this period of Mercian domination, which lasted till AD 655, that groups of Mercian settlers travelled north and established colonies just south of Bradford in the Halifax-Hebden Bridge area. It is in this region that quite a few Mercian place names are found in an area predominantly Anglian.

Penda was killed in AD 655 when he cornered Oswi, a nephew of Edwin, at a place called Winwaed, believed to be Winn Moor, near Leeds. Oswi had been fighting a guerrilla-type war against Penda since his invasion of Northumbria and Penda forced him to a decisive battle at Winn Moor, where he thought he had Oswi trapped. However, Oswi's superior military skill and better knowledge of the terrain helped him defeat Penda, who was killed in the battle.

About 300 years after the arrival of the Angles in the Bradford area another invasion by Germanic peoples took place. This time the invaders came from more northerly areas of Europe, regions that are the modern countries of Denmark and Norway. The new settlers were the Viking Norsemen whose language and customs were added to the existing ones.

The earliest Viking raid on England was recorded in AD 787 in Dorset, but the raids and subsequent settlements in Yorkshire did not develop until the following century. Danish Vikings settled the East and North Ridings, but the majority of Viking settlers who colonised the Yorkshire Dales and further south around Bradford were Norwegian Vikings. These Norsemen had come down the west coast of Scotland, founding settlements there, and also in Ireland, from where they travelled to the west coast of England and then through the Pennines to Craven and the West Riding.

Abundant evidence of Norse settlement around Bradford is again found in place names. The suffixes '-by', '-thwaite', '-toft', '-holme', '-ings' and '-thorpe' are Norse words, often fused with Anglian words, since Old English and Old Norse were cousin languages and their speakers would not have much difficulty in understanding one another.

Examples of this alliance of Norse and Anglian words in Bradford place names are: Hall Ings, which means 'hall in the meadow'; Holmes Street, from the Old Norse *holmr* meaning 'a water meadow'; Skinner Lane, from Old English *lane* and old Norse *skinnari*, meaning a tanner or skinner; Odsal, Oddr's nook of land.

Place names which are entirely Norse in origin are: Legrams, from Old Norse *leith*, meaning 'a road, track' and *grima*, meaning 'a mark on a tree' i.e. a signpost or track indicator; Scholemoor meant 'a moor with a shed, shelter' from *skali*, a shed, shieling; Kirkgate meant 'the church road', from Old Norse *kirk* a church and *gata*, a road.

Other place names which were derived from Anglo-Norse words in use until much later times are: Ivegate, named from the road over the old Ive Bridge which was covered in ivy; Stott Hill, derived from an Old English word *stot*, a horse for drawing carts; Barkerend, the end of the village where tanners lived; Delf Hill, quarry hill; Lidget Green, the green with a 'hlid gat', i.e. a swing-gate on it; Thiefscore, the ford where thieves skulked.

The dialects of Yorkshire still retain strong influences from the Anglo-Norse period. The flat vowels of the Yorkshireman, the way he forms his sentences and the rhythm of his speech all originate from the languages spoken by his Anglo-Norse forebears. Around the Bradford area such dialect words as 'beck', 'fell', 'laithe' (a hayloft), 'barn' (a baby) are all Norse in origin. Words of action such as 'to laike', meaning 'to play', and 'to lig', meaning 'to lie down', or 'to smittle', meaning 'to infect', all stem from the language of the Viking settlers and have their counterparts in modern Danish and Norwegian, although they are absent from Standard English.

The Norsemen were efficient administrators and reorganised the areas they settled in. Bradford did not belong to the Anglo-Saxon administrative divisions of land called a 'hundred', found in the Midlands and South, but to a Norse 'Wapentake'. The Wapentake meant literally 'a taking of weapons', which in turn derived from the number of fighting men who could be mustered in a particular area, or the weapons brandished at a meeting to signify a vote. The

Wapentakes conducted much local administrative business and also acted as courts of justice. Bradford was in the Wapentake of Morley, whereas Leeds and Bingley were in the Wapentakes of Skyrack. Smaller courts within the Wapentake were known as 'Things' and there would be several Things in the Bradford area as part of its administration. The Wapentakes were grouped together in 'Thriddings', each Thridding being a third of the 'Scire', the Shire, which the Norsemen found in Yorkshire too large to organise as one single unit; hence the Thriddings, later to become the Ridings.

The Vikings of the North, which included Bradford, retained a fiercely independent attitude in governing their own affairs. They rebelled constantly against southern domination even when their kingdom had been made a vassal state under the Anglo-Saxon king Edred in AD 954. They rose against King Harold who defeated them at Stamford Bridge in 1066, just before he, in turn, was defeated by William the Conqueror at Hastings. It was not until King William laid waste the North in 1069 that they were in any way subject to a national overlord when the Conqueror built a network of castles to hold them in subjection.

chapter three

'A Praty Quik Market Toune': Medieval and Early Bradford

(John Leland, 1536. 'Quik' = Lively)

The Anglo-Saxon Chronicle for the year 1069 shows only too well the reasons for William's march north. The three years following his invasion in 1066 had been troublesome times in regions away from his main armies. The North had for years opposed any national control as many of those living there were closer in blood and culture to Norway and Denmark than to the peoples living in southern England. In 1069 many Yorkshire Norse earls revolted against William's rule and attacked his garrison at York. Danish Vikings came to help their kinsmen, just as Norwegian Vikings had sailed to Yorkshire three years earlier to help their kinsmen in the abortive attempt to overthrow King Harold at Stamford Bridge.

When news of yet another uprising, this time more serious than any other, reached William, he marched north. Having put the invading Danish force to flight, he then began to burn and destroy villages and settlements between the Humber and the Tees. Once and for all he wished to assert his authority over the natives. Most of the settlements around Bradford were razed to the ground – made waste – as a retaliatory measure by William.

Yet William's 'Harrowing of the North' was not as vicious as some earlier historians have made it out to be. He was too shrewd a ruler to antagonise for any length of time the native people, who were probably only too glad to have a firm ruler bring stability to a country torn by internal feuding for over a century. In any case, it is doubtful whether he would have had enough troops to rule the whole of the country if the majority of the population had been against him. William was selective in the areas he razed. Even where the settlement was razed, as in Bradford's case, life soon returned to normal. Bradford was granted a charter to hold a market less than seventy years after its destruction.

Another pointer to the collaboration of the native population with William is the fact that Anglo-Norse noblemen were often made grants of land. The main new landowners were, of course, the French nobility who had served William during and after his invasion. But even Earl Gospatric, who is cited as joining the Danish forces in 1069, was allowed to hold land directly under William. His former extensive territories in Yorkshire, which included Bingley, Baildon and other local places, were much reduced though, for according to Domesday Book land all over Yorkshire was taken from him and given to others.

Bradford's fate was probably on account of the strong Norse settlements there which had joined the rebellion against William. Most of the names of the former owners of the land listed in Domesday Book seem to be Norse rather than Anglian. It seems a possibility that the Anglian element welcomed William's firm rule. Certainly land was apportioned to native English who became sub-tenants of the Norman overlord. In the Domesday Book register for Mirfield, not far from Bradford, the account reads: 'In Mirfield Gerneber, Haldene, and Gamel had six caracutes of land to be taxed, where there may be 3 ploughs. Three Englishmen now have [them] of Ilbert.'

Mirfield was one of very few manors (holdings of land) which were not razed in the Wapentake of Morley, in which the manor of Bradford lay. In general the Wapentakes of the West Riding seem to have suffered more than those in the East Riding as far as William's policy of devastation was concerned. Perhaps William was shrewd enough to realise that he would be destroying good farms if he razed East Riding settlements. The Pennine Hills, anyhow, were more likely to harbour traditionally hostile and vigorously independent people, as we have seen in earlier periods of their history.

William gave much of the Pennine land to one of his Norman subordinates, Ilbert de Lacy, whose name appears in the reference to the manor of Mirfield above. As well as being the Norman overlord, he was very much a military governor, being ultimately responsible to the king for keeping the land in order. There is evidence that he was not happy with this responsibility at first, though he was a good administrator. His lands stretched from Lincolnshire to Lancashire and his two main strongholds were at Lincoln and Pontefract.

With typical efficiency William set about surveying his new realm once he had subdued it. He wanted to know how much it was worth in terms of wealth and taxes. Teams of commissioners went to the shires with instructions to obtain information from priests, bailiffs and stewards of the manors, and six men from each town and village. The findings for Bradford are noted below. (The spelling is modern. A 'caracute' was roughly 120 acres, a 'berewick' is land suitable for growing corn, and a 'soke' is a division of a manor.)

Manor. In Tuinc [Tong] Stainulf had four caracutes of land to be taxed, where there may be two ploughs. Ilbert has it but it is waste. Value in King Edward's time twenty shillings. Wood pasture half a mile long, and half broad.

Manor. In Dreslintone [Drighlington] Dunstan had four caracutes of land to be taxed, where there may be seven ploughs. Ilbert has it and it is waste. Value in King

Edward's time twenty shillings. Wood pasture four quarentens [half a mile] long, and the same broad.

2 Manors. In Gomershale [Gomersal] Dunstan and Gamel had fourteen caracutes of land to be taxed, where there may be seven ploughs. Ilbert has it and it is waste. Value in King Edward's time forty shillings. Wood pasture one mile long and one broad.

Manor. In Bradeford with six berewicks, Gamel had fifteen caracutes of land to be taxed, where there may be eight ploughs. Ilbert has it and it is waste. Value in King Edward's time four pounds. Wood pasture half a mile long, and half broad.

Manor. In Bodeltone [Bolton] Archil had four caracutes of land to be taxed, where there may be two ploughs. Ilbert has it and it is waste. Value in King Edward's time ten shillings.

This land belongs to this manor: Celeslau [Chellow], Alretone [Allerton], Torentone [Thornton], Claitone [Clayton], Wibertese [Wibsey]. To be taxed together ten caracutes of land, and there may be six ploughs there. It is waste. Value in King Edward's time forty shillings.

Manor. In Bollinc [Bowling] Sindi had four caracutes of land to be taxed, where there may be two ploughs. Ilbert has it, and it is waste. Value in King Edward's time five shillings.

Manor. In Scipeleia [Shipley] Ravenshil had three caracutes of land to be taxed where there may be two ploughs. Ilbert has it and it is waste. Value in King Edward's time ten shillings. Wood pasture one mile long and half broad.

Manor. In Birle [Bierley] Stainulf had four caracutes of land to be taxed, where there may be two ploughs. Ilbert has it and it is waste. Value in King Edward's time ten shillings. Wood pasture half a mile long and half broad.

2 Manors. In Wiche [Wyke] Stainulf and Westre had four caracutes of land to be taxed, where there may be two ploughs. Ilbert has it and it is waste. Value in King Edward's time twenty shillings. Wood pasture four quarentens long and four broad.

2 Manors. In Hetone [Heaton] Dunstan and Ravenshil had six caracutes of land to be taxed, where there may be three ploughs. Ilbert now has it and it is waste. Value in King Edward's time twenty shillings.

Once King William had established his authority in the county, he consolidated his position by building several strongholds where an armed Norman force could be held to maintain law and order. Some indication of the unsettled state of the entire neighbourhood around Bradford may be gained from the number of castles the Normans built in this part of the West Riding. As well as the castle at Pontefract there were castles at Sandal, Cawood, Hazelwood, Harewood, Knaresborough, Ripley, Barden and Skipton.

With the establishment of Norman French power in the country came French learning, customs and the French language. The older monasteries, the country's centres of learning, were taken over by French abbots and the new monasteries which were established, such as that at Kirkstall, were designed and governed by French monks. It is not surprising, then, that the very language of the inhabitants of the hamlet of Bradford, and the surrounding Anglo-Norse hamlets such as Bowling, Frizinghall, Heaton and Wyke, all now suburbs of the city, should begin to undergo change. English remained the language of the land, but the language of literature, the law, the castle and the king's palace was French, while Latin remained the language of the Church.

The language spoken by the Anglo Norse sub-tenants and serfs would still be dialect, for there was no standard language till the fifteenth century. Their dialect was the descendant speech of their Anglo-Norse forebears but it changed in pronunciation during the medieval period and its vocabulary was widened considerably by the addition of Norman-French words. Many Norman-French words have come down into standard English; such words as pork, mutton, beef, castle, prison and jury. Other Norman-French words have disappeared from the standard language, but are still retained in Bradford dialect; such words as chamer (bedroom), arran (a spider), barlow or barley (the children's word for first choice or neutral), coit (a hut) and to galivant (to act blithely).

The Twelfth Century

Rather more quickly than is generally assumed, Bradford recovered from the devastation the Normans inflicted on it, so that by 1147 there appears the first record of the granting of the right to hold a market in his manor of Bradford to the de Lacy overlord. It was a right he would welcome from the king because he would be able to extract taxes from any goods sold there. In 1150 monks from Rievaux Abbey were working iron from land in Bradford which had been given to their monastery, and in 1170 a church at Tong (St James' Church) was consecrated. All these events took place less than a hundred years after Domesday Book was compiled and they would indicate a quick return of population around Bradford after the scorched-earth policy of King William. The size of Bradford's population at this time would be less than 300 people, counting the inhabitants of the surrounding hamlets which fell within the pre-1974 city's boundaries.

What was life like in the manors around Bradford during medieval times? To begin with the area covered by the city today held a collection of tiny hamlets, quite separate from each other and in their own manors. The de Lacy family sub-let their lands and the Bolling manor was held by a tenant called William de Bolling, a man of some standing in 1165 when he is recorded as a benefactor of Kirkstall Abbey. Tenants such as the Bollings swore loyalty and paid taxes to their de Lacy overlords, who in turn owed their allegiance to the Crown. There is also a 'castle' mentioned in a medieval document relating to the de Lacy estate at Bradford, but this term was used very loosely and the 'castle' in the manor of Bradford was probably little more than a sizeable stone house. Belonging to the manor was some farmland which would be tilled by under-tenants of several kinds. All of the farmhands and under-tenants would be of Anglo-Norse stock, and their new overlords would be mainly Norman-French, and only occasionally English.

Of the farm-hands or under-tenants, the sokeman was the most independent and held land by paying rents directly to his overlord. Serfs or villeins were not independent but were tied to their lord's lands and had to work on them in return for protection from the lord. The villein was, in fact, part of the estate and was not allowed to leave his lord's manor without the lord's permission, nor could he permit his sons to enter the priesthood, nor his daughters to marry, without permission of the overlord.

Sometimes other services than work on his lord's lands were performed by the under-tenant. Certain lands were held in Manningham in the fourteenth century on condition that the tenant helped his overlord to hunt wild boar in the area and blew the hunter's horn. Very probably the job he had to do was act as kennel-master and look after a pack of hounds, a job which would have taken up the time the tenant might have spent working on the lord's lands.

The Thirteenth Century

By the middle of the thirteenth century Bradford must have been a valuable possession for the de Lacys. There was a thriving community living there, industrious and productive. A chapel or small church had already been built, for in a deed of 1220 is mentioned a priest living at Bradford, and there is also mention of a priest (clericus) of Allerton in a deed of 1200. In 1241 the church had become important enough for a 'rector' to be appointed, and five years later the manor of Bradford was sufficiently thriving to be taxed at five marks for the King's Tax. The best indication of the growth of the medieval village is the granting in 1251 of another charter for the manor to hold a market; a market that the John Street market is the descendent of today.

Medieval names still in existence show the growth of this early centre of Bradford. They reveal some of the trades carried on in the community then. Colliergate was the road down which coal would be brought from the bell pits worked on the moors above medieval Bradford. Hustlergate was the road of pickpockets while Barkerend was the street of the medieval tanners and Skinner Lane the place where slaughtered beasts were skinned. Other street names which exist from the medieval village are: Cheapside, Church Bank, Kirkgate,

The Market Cross today resides in the Kirkgate Market. The plaque reads: 'The Bradford Market was first held in 1251 in the vicinity of the Parish Church (now the cathedral). It was later removed to the bottom of Westgate where it was held for many centuries until 1801. The Market Place in Westgate was the triangular opening at the top of Kirkgate and Ivegate. An ancient market cross stood not far from the top of Ivegate. During the Civil War the top of the cross was said to have been broken off by the overzealous Puritans in their desire to obliterate all traces of the faith which they so stoutly condemned.'

Hall Ings, Ivegate, Manor Row, Market Street, Northgate, Westgate, Southgate and Pit Lane. They indicate just where the original village of Bradford lay and show the extent of its development.

In 1277 an Inquisition was taken of Bradford; that is, a survey was made and recorded of Bradford's commerce and population. It gives us a clear insight into the way of life of people in Bradford at that time. The survey tells us that Henry de Lacy had certain privileges in 'the town of Bradeford: to wit, a gallows, assize of bread and beer, a market place and a free court from ancient times'. In other words, the lord of the manor could hang criminals at Bradford, could control and therefore tax the amount of bread and beer made there, could hold a market in Bradford and levy taxes on the goods sold in it, and could hold a local court in the township where fines for minor offences could be levied. Fines were extracted in the form of goods as well as in cash, for the Inquisition lists a fine levied on a Gomersal weaver, the first documentary evidence we have of weaving in Bradford: 'And they [the survey team] say that Nicholas de Burton, Steward of Henry de Lacy, had Evam, weaver of Gomersal, in the prison at Bradeford, and took from him two cows, and permitted him to go without judgement.'

The growth of the medieval community in Bradford is illustrated by references in documents relating to the church there which, in 1292, assess the combined living of the vicar and rector to be £53 6s 8d. The following year a document stipulates that the newly appointed Vicar of Bradford had 'to be in personal residence', i.e. it was a full-time appointment and not one he shared with other parishes. A charter for a five days' annual fair in 1294 also shows the growing importance of Bradford as a commercial centre for the Dales of the West Riding. A Sunday market in the churchyard was also established in 1310.

The Fourteenth Century

When Henry de Lacy died, another Inquisition of Bradford was made in 1311 for an assessment of all Henry's lands, which extended over a vast region of northern England. Bradford came under the jurisdiction of his castle at Pontefract where the Inquisition for this area was carried out. The Inquisition tells us that Henry de Lacy, Earl of Lincoln:

> had at Bradford a hall or manor house, with chambers, and it is nothing worth beyond necessary repairs, and there are forty acres in demesne [farmland], demised to divers tenants at will, and the yearly value is 8d an acre, £1 6s 8d.
> And there is one water mill valued by the year at £10, and a fulling-mill which is worth yearly £1. And there is a certain market every seventh day, upon the Lord's Day, the toll of which is worth yearly £3.
> And there is a certain fair which is held annually upon the Feast of Saint Andrew the Apostle, the toll of which is worth yearly £3. And there are certain villeins who hold twenty three oxgangs of land in bondage, and render yearly, at the Feast of Saint Martin, £4 16s. And the same villeins do work in autumn, which is worth yearly, for every oxgang 3d. [An 'oxgang' is the amount of land an ox could plough in a day.]

John James, the Bradford historian, draws the conclusion from the data given in the 1311 Inquisition that Bradford's population at this time was about 650, though it is very difficult to arrive at an accurate figure which can be compared with the present city. Roughly speaking, it would seem that Bradford's population had doubled from the time of Domesday to the beginning of the fourteenth century, about 220 years.

Another piece of information which can be gleaned from the 1311 Inquisition is that Bradford Parish Church received an endowment of 96 acres of land from its patrons, the de Lacys. It is a further sign of the developing township, which had a permanent rector and vicar by this time, although Bradford Parish Church still paid the original mother church at Dewsbury the sum of 8s a year.

There are also the names of thirty-two freeholders paying rents, instead of labour, to their overlord. These men were much more independent of the feudal lord's authority than the villeins, who were little more than bondmen. The fact that they could pay money instead of goods or labour meant they were free to develop industry in the medieval township. Many of them did just this and it seems that it was those places with a nucleus of freeholders living in them which developed rapidly as centres of commerce and industry. They had a start over other medieval communities which, centuries later, was to help them develop into the great cities they are today. Another interesting factor concerning the freeholders is their names. Many of those 1311 freeholders names continue to the present as typically Bradfordian personal names like Pollard, Balmer, Thornton and Northrop.

Between 1311 and 1322 the Scots began raiding Yorkshire, especially after the English defeat at Bannockburn in 1314. Their raids became more and more frequent and more destructive, as the defence of England was left to local overlords, who could scarcely contain the organised raiders. In 1314 they ravaged Ilkley and in 1318 burnt Otley Church where the population, as in Bradford, used to take shelter. The monks at Bolton Abbey had to leave their monastery and seek protection in Skipton Castle and in 1318, the church at Bradford was so far damaged that a new one was decided on. The value of the living dropped from £53 in 1292 to £28 after the Scottish raids.

Barely had the township recovered from the Scottish attacks than a more deadly onslaught caused a setback in the growth of Bradford. A series of plagues swept through England between 1342 and 1378, reducing Bradford's population by about a half by the time of the Black Death in 1349. The lot of the Bradford serf at this time could not have been a very happy one, threatened as he was by raiders from over the border and liable to fall victim at any time to one of the plagues ravaging the population. Harry Speight, in the *British Association Handbook* for 1900, gives a vivid account of the condition of one Bradford villein in 1342. He was paid 3s 1½d a year and given 3d for release of harvest work and 1s for pasturing his beasts on the common (so fertilizing it). In return he had to repair the mill dam and, for providing millstones, he received the old millstones, half of the old timber for his services and half a measure of oatmeal. He also had to look after the mill, and furnish a man and horse to carry the de Lacy's food on the lord's journeys from Bradford to his lands in Lancashire. For the latter service he received 4d at each town they passed through. With other serfs he had to carry wood for his lord's works and was paid 12d for every cartload. He was forbidden to give his daughter in marriage or let his son become a priest. Eventually this particular villein became a man of property and the tenant of the soke (corn) mills at Bradford.

In 1361, Henry, Duke of Lancaster, the lord of the manor at Bradford died and the manor passed to his daughter, Blanche. She married John of Gaunt, who held the manor from 1361 to 1399. It was during Gaunt's overlordship that the legend of the Wild Boar of Cliffe Wood is based. It was Gaunt, too, who granted land to John Northrop of Manningham in return for acting as a kind of huntsman for him during his stays in the Bradford area. Later, the horn blowing of Northrop gave rise to a custom involving the blowing of a horn which lasted up to the beginning of the nineteenth century. The boar legend and horn blowing custom are commemorated in the city's coat of arms.

Gaunt was head of the powerful Lancaster faction during Richard II's reign and the headquarters of the Lancasters was Pontefract Castle. The castle was the administrative centre for much of the West Riding's affairs during the Middle Ages. The overlords of the area, starting with the de Lacys and continuing through the Lancaster family, held their assize courts there. When Gaunt died, Pontefract Castle was seized by the king, along with other lands held by Lancaster. The manor of Bradford became part of the Crown lands until Bolingbroke, Gaunt's son who had been exiled by Richard, landed near Hull, at Ravensburgh, and deposed the king. Bolingbroke set himself up as King Henry IV and eventually had Richard II imprisoned, then murdered, at Pontefract Castle.

Richard authorised a Poll Tax to be levied in 1378. Lists were drawn up throughout the country of all persons above sixteen years of age, and the sums which they had to pay to the king according to their station in life. For example, merchants paid anything from 13s 4d to 20s and each single person, not a merchant, paid 4d. The tax was very unpopular in its time but its records give us interesting details of the social life at that time.

In the manor of Bradford itself, twenty-six men and their wives were taxed at sums varying from that of 'Willelmus Burges, Hostiler, et uxor [and wife]' who paid 12d, to 'Thomas Smyth, et uxor' who paid 4d. There were also thirty-four single people taxed, all at 4d. All the other hamlets around Bradford, which are now its suburbs, hamlets such as Manningham, Bowling and Clayton, were taxed in the same manner.

The way the population is named gives us an interesting insight into their professions or places of origin. Surnames fall, broadly speaking, into two categories: occupational surnames and surnames derived from the place of origin. Willelmus Burges, or to give the modern spelling of his name, William Burgess, was an innkeeper. A burgess was a man freed from the serfdom of the villeins and he usually owned his own house and became quite an important local figure in late medieval times. There is a Thomas Walker mentioned who is classified as a fuller. His surname, as we should expect, gives us an indication of his trade, for after cloth was woven it had to be trampled or walked on in water for hours to soften and cleanse it before it was fit for use. Johanna Webster took her name from the weaving trade, for a webster was the medieval term for a weaver. There are surnames denoting the birthplace of the Bradfordians of 1378. Quite a few of them originally came from villages outside the hamlet. The village tailor is a Johannes de Hetton (John of Heaton), and the cobbler is Willelmus filius Thorne (William son of Thorne). Many of the names have modern counterparts. Appleyard, Ledgard, Walker, Harper, Nicholson, Ellis, Barker, Milner, Webster, Sharp, Slater, Perkin and Northrop are names still common in the Bradford area.

The records of the manor court of Bradford during the fourteenth century make interesting reading, too, and show us how the small medieval community fared. In 1347 a tanner was brought before the court for not paying a toll on the leather he made, and another inhabitant was fined for taking peat for fuel from the moors without licence. Ten years later another tanner was fined for polluting Bradford Beck by dumping the refuse of his trade in it and in 1358 and 1360 there are more prosecutions for theft of fuel from the lord's demesne. One interesting point recorded in these latter prosecutions is that the people fined were scratching the surface of the land for outcrop coal and digging shallow pits. Coal-mining developed properly later and it was the good accessibility of coal which helped Bradford to develop as an industrial city in the nineteenth century.

The wool trade in and around Bradford continued to flourish in late medieval times. The medieval village was fortunately placed in the proximity of such great abbeys as Kirkstall and Fountains, while smaller religious houses, such as that at Bolton Abbey, ensured a plentiful supply of raw wool from the monks' outlying sheep farms, the granges higher up the Dales. In 1394 the manufacture of kersies, a piece of narrow woven cloth, is reported as being a very flourishing trade in Bradford; and indeed, the medieval community was admirably situated in the middle of a soft water area for the production of good scoured wool. This, of course, led eventually to the development of all the crafts associated with woollen cloth production such as combing, spinning, weaving and finishing. So important was the maintenance of good water supplies to the community as a whole, that in 1412 a villager of Eccleshill was fined for diverting the village's water supplies to his own use.

The Fifteenth Century

Despite the upheavals of the late medieval period, Bradford continued to develop, primarily as a cloth-producing community. The population decline due to the plagues of the previous century was gradually being made good and the medieval village began to build itself a new parish church in 1431, the third church on the same site. This was completed by 1458. Pontefract and the Lancaster family still governed Bradford's affairs, yet despite the town's allegiance to the Lancastrian faction, Bradford itself was not greatly affected by the Wars of the Roses. The nearest fighting of these wars was at Wakefield, where a detachment of Lancastrians attacked the Yorkist garrison at Sandal Castle in 1460. The bloodiest battle of the wars resulted from this attack, at which the Duke of York was killed, for his son, Edward IV, marched north to avenge his father's death and fought the Lancastrian army, which doubtless contained some Bradford men, at Towton Field, near Tadcaster in 1461. Over 30,000 men were killed.

Towards the end of the fifteenth century, Bradford was a thriving market town. A report compiled on the woollen industry for 1479 lists Bradford as sixth in importance for West Riding manufacturing centres of woollen cloth, following Halifax, Ripon, Almondbury, Leeds and Pontefract. In 1485 the rival York and Lancaster families were united under Henry Tudor (Henry VII) who married a Yorkist wife. Bradford by this time was well-established in the textile trade, with facilities for carrying out all stages in the production of woollen cloth that was needed by a medieval community. It had its own fullers' mills, weavers and finishers, and, just as important, it had its own market and merchants to sell its wares. But the neighbouring village of Manningham seems to have been particularly hard hit by the taxes the new Tudor monarch was imposing on it. Among the documents relating to the manor of Manningham for 1489 is a complaint against the king's bailiff, John Clark, who took common land from the tenants because they could not pay Crown rents.

The Sixteenth Century

Towards the end of the fifteenth century and in the early years of the sixteenth century, Bradford, in common with other towns throughout the country, suffered from the heavy taxes which Henry VII imposed on the population. Since the days of John of Gaunt, the manor of Bradford had been in the possession of the Lancaster family, which became the ruling house on the accession of Henry IV. The Crown had let out the manor to the highest bidder and subsequent Dukes of Lancaster farmed out their lands, too. During Henry VII's reign the bailiff in Bradford for the Chancellor of the Duchy of Lancaster was Raynbron Bolling, who, under the instructions of his master, extorted money so unjustly that in 1503 five Bradford tenants led by Sir Richard Tempest filed a complaint in the Duchy Court against Raynbron Bolling. Trade had fallen off in the township and its citizens were being unjustly fined as the complaint shows:

> ... there were three fairs at Bradford, of great resort of merchants, pedlars and chapmen [hawkers], and of the inhabitants of the surrounding country ... such fairs, by reason of the excessive and unlawful toll demanded by the bailiff, are much less attended, and the town thereby greatly hurt ... the said bailiff taketh and driveth cattle off the grounds of the King's tenants at Bradford and secreteth them in remote parts of the parish, and then after a time claims them as waifs [strays] ... in the sixteenth year of Henry VII [1501], he caused certain women to shear twenty sheep of the King's tenants at Bradford so that they were not known again ... on the fifth of June, in the seventeenth year of Henry VII [1502], he took from Ellen, late wife of Tristram Bolling, five ewes; from Elizabeth Bristow, two cows and from William Wright, a cow ... one William Gordon, a Scotch chapman, who was coming from Halifax with three packs of wool, was waylaid by the said bailiff upon Manningham Moor, because the said chapman ought to have come through Bradford and paid toll, and cast him down and beat him, and caused him to pay 6s 8d and above in money.

One interesting factor which comes out of the complaint Sir Richard Tempest made against the bailiff Bolling is the influence the church still possessed in the area. A considerable part of the area around Bradford was held by the great abbeys of Yorkshire, which had originally been granted land, for the most part waste and uncultivated, early in the Norman period. The Abbot of Kirkstall, who owned land in Horton, was selected as a judge in the Court of Bradford and thus shows he was still a person of some note and authority in the area. He was controller of the nunnery at Esholt, whose grounds now lie within Bradford's boundaries. His authority as an influential person in the area would last until the Dissolution of the Monasteries in Henry VIII's reign, some thirty years later. Other great religious houses in the vicinity which were stripped of their lands and wealth by Henry VIII were the priories at Bolton in Wharfedale, Nostell near Wakefield, and Kirklees near Huddersfield. There was a large Cluniac monastery at Pontefract, as well as the Cistercian abbeys at Kirkstall and Fountains. Drax Abbey, near Selby, also held land in the Bradford area, as did the Knights Templars at Temple Newsam, near Leeds.

The greatest advantage Bradford had from its proximity to these great religious houses would be a plentiful supply of raw material to draw on for the development of its wool trade. Kirkstall Abbey was especially famous for the quality of the wool it produced on the granges it farmed in the dales around Bradford, and doubtless some of the cloth produced from this wool was woven in Bradford and sold at its fairs and markets.

In 1536, Bradford was visited by John Leland, a chaplain of Henry VIII, who made an itinerary of the country and reported what he saw to the king. Leland describes Bradford as 'a praty quik [lively] market toune ... smaller than Wakefield. It hath one paroche churche and a chapel of Saint Sitha. It standith much by clothing and is distant six miles from Halifax and four miles from Kirkstall Abbey'. Leeds at that time is described as being 'as large as Bradeforde, but not so quik'.

In 1534 Henry VIII made his historic break with Rome and Protestantism became the official religion of the country. After 1534 Henry set about crushing the power of the Roman Catholic Church which was vested primarily in the great abbeys and monasteries up and down the country. Already in 1530 the convent at Esholt, founded on land given by Simon de Ward to Kirkstall Abbey in the middle of the twelfth century, was abolished with smaller religious houses, and ten years later the monks from Kirkstall were driven from their abbey, which was stripped of its lead roof and its stone used for constructing a bridge over the River Aire.

In 1536 the king met opposition to his suppression of Catholicism in Yorkshire, especially after his closure of powerful religious houses in York. Many Roman Catholic nobles in the area of Bradford joined the rebellion of the Yorkshireman Robert Aske in his Pilgrimage of Grace against Henry. Nicholas Tempest of Bolling Hall was deeply implicated and was executed for his opposition to the king, as was Lord Darcy, the owner of Temple Newsam and Pontefract Castle. The Clifford family, however, further up Airedale at Skipton Castle, were staunch Protestants and held out against the rebel forces surrounding them.

Closely linked with the Parish Church history in Bradford during Tudor times is the history of Bradford Grammar School. The school is first mentioned in a document of 1553, the beginning of the reign of Queen Mary, but it is highly probable some sort of school had been in existence much earlier, for grammar schools had been founded throughout Yorkshire during Tudor times. The Tudor reigns coincided with the English Renaissance: the rebirth of Classical learning and the advent of modern science out of the superstitious guesswork of the Middle Ages. It also marked an expansion in English commerce when a wider educated class of merchants was needed to develop trade. Consequently, numerous schools were established to meet this demand for a better educated class.

One factor which facilitated this rapid founding of so many schools around Bradford was the easier access schools had to books. The invention of the printing press, which also was an influence in the standardizing of the language from a complex series of dialects, did away with the laborious copying out by hand of each book, the shortage of which naturally limited the number of schools using them and tended to confine learning to the places where handwritten books were produced, the monasteries. The spread of learning was also hindered by this expensive and slow method of book production. In 1509, about twenty-five years after Caxton had established his printing press at Westminster, Hugo Goes set up a printing press in York. As far as we know, his was the first one built in Yorkshire and it is significant that so many Tudor grammar schools, including Bradford Grammar School, were founded soon after the establishing of the press at York.

In 1553 a lawsuit in the Duchy Court about whether the Crown had rights to certain lands in Bradford mentions rents 'which anciently belonged to the living and sustentation of a schoolmaster teaching grammar within the town of Bradford'. Ten years later, a former Vicar of Bradford, Thomas Ockden, left in his will dated 1563 a legacy to 'Robert Hall, schoolmaister of the school at Bradeforde, for such paynes as he hath taken for me'. Both these documents establish the founding of a grammar school in Tudor times and possibly earlier.

The Crown began to take more and more interest in the lands of the West Riding as the great expansion of textile activity took place in the sixteenth century. Until the sixteenth century the North, in comparison with the rest of England, was a backwater, especially in regions about the Pennines where there was poor arable land and a sparse population paying little in taxes. The Crown, therefore, had scanty interest in it until the growth of its industries made it more valuable as a source of revenue. In 1580 Sir Richard Tempest of Bolling Hall had to prove his ownership of the manor of Allerton in a suit in the Duchy Court brought against him by Queen Elizabeth. The queen was trying to recover Allerton for the Crown on the grounds that it was part of the manor of Bradford. Tempest won his case against the Crown by proving his rights to the land in a decree which gives some interesting facts about the history of the Bolling, Thornton and Tempest families, three of Bradford's oldest families.

Judgement was given against the claims of Queen Elizabeth on the grounds that the matters alleged to support her claim to the waste grounds of Allerton were not sufficient proof to counterbalance the evidence of Sir Richard Tempest.

Judgement also decreed that Tempest and his heirs should henceforth be entitled to hold 'the said lands, wastes and water corn mill, also 236 acres of land in Allerton, until better proof be shown for their not holding the same on behalf of Her Majesty'. Four years later, in 1584, the first enclosure of the waste or common land in Allerton and Wilsden 'were confirmed in rights of pasture and liberty to dig and get stones, with power to enclose and improve the said moors, commons and waste'.

Queen Elizabeth was recognising the growing prosperity of the West Riding. The area as a whole had increased in wealth tremendously since the reign of her grandfather a century previously. She taxed woollen products heavily and discovered that Bradford, in 1594, was the centre of a cushion-making industry which had escaped her broad cloth tax. She passed an ordinance taxing at once all manufactures of wool clothing except such parts as were worn for personal use by the cloth manufacturers and their families. But she also aided the textile industry in Bradford by decreeing that 'all persons above the age of seven years shall wear upon the Sabbath and Holy Days upon their heads, a cap of wool, knit, thicked and dressed in England, upon pain of forfeit, for every day not wearing, three shillings and fourpence'.

The fortunes of the Tempest family fluctuated wildly during the Tudor period. The connection of the family with Bolling Hall began in Henry VII's reign when the last of the Bolling family lived there. Tristram Bolling married his daughter Rosamund to the first Richard Tempest. Tristram then went to live at Chellow Grange in Heaton.

The first Richard Tempest rose high in the early part of Henry VIII's reign, holding a command of troops at the Battle of Flodden (1513) and becoming High Sheriff of Yorkshire in 1516. Later in Henry's reign the Tempests fell into disfavour and Richard Tempest's son, Nicholas, was executed for his opposition to Henry's break with Rome and the Dissolution of the Monasteries. The Tempests fell into disfavour again when the Protestant Queen Elizabeth came to the throne, but there is some evidence that they had oppressed the inhabitants of Bradford, as stewards of the manor, by unjust taxation and seizure of common land – the very crime of the bailiff Raynbron Bolling which the first Richard Tempest had complained so bitterly about to Henry VII!

Queen Elizabeth set up a commission headed by Sir Thomas Gargrave to enquire into the amount of common land the Tempests had encroached upon in Bradford since the beginning of Henry VIII's reign, when the Tempests had been made stewards of Bradford. As a result of the commission's findings the stewardship of Bradford was taken from the Tempests and given to the Saviles of Howley Hall, who remained stewards throughout Elizabeth's reign and until the manor was granted out in Charles I's reign.

The fortunes of the Tempest family reached their lowest ebb in the next century, when, after having to sell many of his lands through spendthrift habits, the last Tempest, a Richard, died in London's Fleet Prison in 1657. He had joined the Royalists at the outbreak of the Civil War in the 1640s and when the

Royalist Earl of Newcastle besieged Bradford in 1643, Richard Tempest allowed his home, Bolling Hall, to be used as the Royalist headquarters, a fact which went heavily against him when Parliamentary supremacy was established. When Charles II came to the throne, the Bolling estate had passed into the hands of the Lindley family.

Early Seventeenth-Century Bradford

The Parish Church registers, begun in the reign of Queen Elizabeth, show that at the end of the Tudor period, Bradford and Leeds were very much the same size. In the first thirty years of the seventeenth century, however, the town of Leeds surged ahead of Bradford in growth and county importance.

Several factors were responsible for the sudden development of Leeds. Geographically, it was better placed than Bradford as a market town, being served by a bigger road network and lying on a river that was navigable by flat-bottomed craft down to the Humber. The Cloth Market of Leeds held on the Aire Bridge at the bottom of Briggate was also widely known as a dispersal point for finished cloth made in all parts of the West Riding. There was another factor, too, which influenced the development of Leeds, and that was the efforts Sir John Savile and a group of merchants exerted to develop the township.

On the accession of James I to the throne in 1603, the manors of Leeds and Bradford formed part of the Duchy of Lancaster still. They belonged to the Crown and were administered through a bailiff, a local citizen of importance, as steward to keep an eye on the day-to-day running of the manors. The steward of both manors was Sir John Savile in James I's reign and that of his son, Charles I.

From a survey of the manors in 1612, we know that Leeds and Bradford had been given as a marriage gift to James I's wife, Anne of Denmark. The queen, as overlord, exercised her authority through her steward in three courts: (a) the Court-leet for trying criminal offenders, (b) the Court-baron for managing the affairs of the town in roughly the same way a modern council does, and (c) the Court of frank-pledge for keeping order in the town by seeing that its citizens were properly divided into suitable groups responsible for each other's actions.

The affairs of Leeds seem to have attracted Savile more than the affairs of Bradford, possibly because there was living in Leeds a larger nucleus of wealthy merchants. Sir John Savile lived at Rowley Hall, near Morley, and it is from his family crest that the owls are taken which now form part of the coat of arms of the City of Leeds.

Sir John was an influential courtier in both the courts of James I and Charles I, being six times Member of Parliament for Yorkshire and becoming Baron Savile of Pontefract in 1628, two years before his death. He played an important part in negotiating the buying of the manor of Bradford from the Crown in 1628, and the manor of Leeds in the 1630s. By these moves, both Leeds and Bradford

43

achieved more independence from the Crown in administering their own civic affairs, an independence which enabled them to expand rapidly at the onset of the Industrial Revolution in the late eighteenth century.

The survey of the manor of Bradford in 1612 shows the extent to which it stretched at the beginning of the seventeenth century and the fines and taxes which were paid to the Crown. The terms by which tenants and their heirs held land are also laid down and the jurors, the leading citizens, testifying before the head of the Crown Commission, Sir William Inglegye, stipulate:

> ... that his Majesty is sole lord of Bradford, Manningham and Stanbury, and hath rents and services of his freeholders within the towns and hamlets following, apertaining [sic] to the said manor – Horton, Clayton, Thornton, Allerton, Wilsden, Oxenhope and Haworth – that there is divers [sic] lands in Bradford very anciently granted as copyhold lands, and amounting to 218 acres 3 roods ... [The jurors say] there is no timber, wood or trees growing upon any of the said copyhold lands, only in hedgerows, which they [the tenants] use to cut down for repairing of their tenements; but for mines of stone, coal or metal, they know of none in the same.
>
> And they further say that there is a certain moor, waste or common in Bradford, containing 150 acres, or thereabouts, which is reported as followeth – to wit, upon the middle of certain closes called the Lady Closes, belonging to the Free School of Bradford, on the west part; upon one great old casten ditch, and certain meer stones, situate [sic] between Bradford and Eccleshill, on the north part; upon Waynforth Clough on the east part; and upon the desmesnes of Tyersal on the south part; which said common is very unfruitful ground, and great part spoiled by highways; upon which common his Majesty's freeholders and copyholders of Bradford used to have common of pasture and turbary [right to gather fuel] time out of mind. And they further say that there is a certain mine of stone upon it, out of which divers freeholders have gotten, and constantly used to get, stone for building and repairing their tenements.

John James, in his history of Bradford, draws attention to the kind of daily life being lived in Bradford which can be gathered from surviving copies of court cases in Tudor and Stuart times. In the records of the Court-leet, held bi-annually, he instances the number of women fined for brawling in Bradford. The fine for an assault where no blood was drawn was 3s 4d. A bloody brawl resulted in then heavy fine of 10s. Citizens were fined for eavesdropping, for using obscene language, or for simply being bad neighbours. The puritanical nature of Bradford's Jacobean magistrates is reflected in the fines they imposed for gambling, especially at cards. Two Bradford citizens were fined for playing bowls in Elizabeth's reign, though doubtless there were some side bets going on at the same time!

In common with many other Elizabethan towns, Bradford kept any vagrant persons on the move and refused permission to people wanting to settle within its boundaries who might be a potential drain on its resources. It was ordered in the Leet-court 'that no person do entertain a stranger, without the consent of the constable and four freeholders under their hands, upon pain of 39s 11d every month'. A certain Ann Clough and her child, 'who have come from near Woodchurch' were ordered to be out of the town in ten days 'upon pain of l2d a day if they continue longer'. Fines were also imposed for craftsmen taking in apprentices without the churchwardens' leave, and other people were fined for taking in lodgers illegally. The hiring of young men as servants was also prohibited, only labourers, employed on a day-to-day basis, being permitted.

The ordinary citizen of Bradford, then, was pretty heavily imposed on during the early part of the seventeenth century. He also had to repair the road opposite his house and the packhorse highways crossing his land, with heavy fines being inflicted on those going in default. In 1602 seven people were fined 3s 4d each for not grinding their corn at the manorial soke mill, where the miller himself was fined, along with other citizens, for casting ashes into the Bradford Beck from which much of the domestic water supply was taken.

The rural nature of Bradford in the early seventeenth century is especially illustrated by the court records. Fines were exacted for pigs being allowed to go loose un-ringed about the town. People were also fined for keeping diseased horses and scabbed cattle. Immediate distraints followed on the wrong-doers if they could not pay their fines.

Bradford During the Civil War and Commonwealth

Two outstanding factors which caused civil war to break out in 1642 were Charles I's dogmatic High Church views, which were regarded as Popery in the more moderate Protestant areas where he tried to impose his views, and his harsh tax levies, often imposed unfairly, which forced a growing merchant class in the new industrial areas like the West Riding townships to seek redress against the Crown by taking up arms against it. Bradford suffered on both accounts. In religion it inclined to extreme Protestantism, almost to Puritanism, for as well as the Anglican Church being 'Low Church' by 1642, a dissenters' church, the Moravian Church, had been opened in Little Horton in 1638. Bradford woolmen were also heavily taxed by Charles and inclined strongly to Parliament's cause when the rift opened between the king and Parliament.

The Civil War was, in many ways, a struggle between two sets of leaders in the country: the Low Church, puritanical merchant class against the High Church landed gentry. Bradford fell firmly into the former category, although its older aristocratic families, like the Tempests and Saviles, joined the Royalist cause. The values of the landed aristocracy meant little to the new merchant class developing in Bradford, a merchant class which had become increasingly hostile to the Crown since James I's time. James I had granted monopolies to extract money from the growing industries of the West Riding and he had given one Yorkshire wool merchant, Alderman Cockayne, the sole right of exporting cloth at the expense of his fellow woolmen and to the benefit of the Crown. James' son, Charles I, made the situation worse by his unfair levying of ship money in 1636 and by his attempts at suppressing Low Church clergy in Bradford.

We have a very interesting account of conditions in Bradford during the Civil War and afterwards in the autobiography of a Bradford man who lived at the time. He was Joseph Lister, born in 1627 and therefore only a lad of fifteen or so when the Civil War first affected Bradford. Nevertheless, he presents us with a very vivid, if sometimes biased, account of how Bradford people fared in those violent days. Joseph Lister belonged to a group of dissenting churchmen at Kipping, near Thornton, so, as we can expect, his account of Bradford during the Civil War is highly coloured in favour of the extreme Protestants. He does, however, show us just how tragically the country was divided during the Civil War, when families were often split, one side set against the other. Lister tells us of the migration to America of many Puritans from Bradford just before hostilities commenced. He is quite vituperative in his account of Charles I, which shows us an opinion of the Crown held by many Bradford citizens at that time:

> King Charles the First, then upon the throne, to say nothing of his own wicked disposition, did by the constant solicitation of the bloody Queen, together with the swarms of Jesuits and evil affected Councellors, Bishops, and men of great estate, place, and trust, all put their heads together to destroy Christ's interest in the nation, and betray their trust every way to the utter ruin and overthrow of Religion, and to cut off the lives of all the protestants, and so have enslaved this land to Rome, the mother of harlots; whose kingdom is established by blood.

Bradford was involved very early on in the war and the first encounter of any note was fought within the township. On Sunday 18 December 1642, Bradford was attacked by a group of Royalists from Leeds headed by Sir William Savile, former Steward of Bradford Manor. Savile's attack was beaten off.

One of the early major battles of the Civil War was also fought just outside Bradford at Adwalton Moor, on 30 June 1643. The Parliamentary forces under Lord Fairfax and his son, Sir Thomas Fairfax, were defeated there by the Royalist's leader, the Earl of Newcastle. In his memoirs, Sir Thomas Fairfax writes:

> ... we had held up nearly two years against a potent [Royalist] army, but they finding us now almost tired with continual service, treacherously used by friends, and wanting many things necessary for support and defence, the Earl of Newcastle marched with an army of ten or twelve thousand men to besiege ... Bradford, which was a very untenable place ... We resolved next morning very early with a party of three thousand men to attempt his [Newcastle's] whole army, as they lay in their quarters three miles off, hoping by it to put him into some distraction which could not by reason of the unequal number be done in any other way.

The Fairfaxes lost the Battle of Adwalton Moor. Lord Fairfax retired to Leeds with part of his army, and his son, Sir Thomas Fairfax, went via Halifax into Bradford which Newcastle promptly besieged. Eventually, when the defenders were down to their last barrel of powder, Sir Thomas decided to cut his way through the besieging Royalists and join the Parliamentary troops at Leeds.

Bradford was captured by the Earl of Newcastle on 2 July and the Royalists entered the town, pillaging the houses but not killing many of the inhabitants according to Lister: 'Some desperate fellows wounded several persons, that died of their wounds afterwards; but I think not more than half a score were slain; and that was a wonder, considering what hatred and rage they came against us'.

Lister, who would have been sixteen at the time, escaped from Bradford and went to Colne to find his employer, who had taken the Parliamentary side and fled there after the Royalist victory. His employer sent him back to Bradford to seek his mother and Lister gives us this graphic account of Bradford during its Royalist occupation:

> So in the morning he sent me away, and to Bradford I came, and found some few people left, but most of them scattered and fled away. I lodged in a cellar that night, but oh! what a change was made in the town in three days' time! Nothing was left to eat or drink, or lodge upon, the streets being full of chaff and feathers and meal, the enemies having emptied all the town of what was worth carrying away, and were now sat down and encamped near Bowling Hall, and there kept a fair and sold the things that would sell ... The women were gathering meal in the streets; for when the soldiers found anything that was better than meal, they emptied the sacks, and put that which was better into them, so that there was good store of meal thrown out, both in the houses and streets.

From time to time, as old buildings have been pulled down to make way for new ones, relics of the sieges and attacks on Bradford have been found. Cannonballs and shot from the guns especially have turned up as mementos from the Civil War in succeeding centuries, while Bolling Hall, the headquarters of the Royalists, is now a museum in its own right and contains many interesting features connected with this period of Bradford's history.

Throughout the Civil War the wool towns in the West Riding were occupied first by the Royalists, then by the Parliamentarians. General Lambert soon recovered Bradford and repelled a further Royalist attack, and a victory of the Fairfaxes at Selby in 1644 enabled them to join the Scots at Tadcaster and besiege the Earl of Newcastle at York. Prince Rupert came to relieve him and eventually made the Parliamentary forces, who had been joined by the Earl of Manchester and Oliver Cromwell's troops, withdraw a short way off. The Royalists then forced a battle at Marston Moor on 2 July 1644, but they were defeated and their leaders had to flee the country.

By the orders of Parliament, castles which had held out for the Royalists were demolished, and around Bradford, the castles at Pontefract, Knaresborough, Sandal and Barden Tower were dismantled. Skipton Castle was also partially demolished.

Late Seventeenth-Century Bradford

Under pressure from the Royalists and High Church faction, Puritanism in Bradford became ever more popular during the early stages of the Civil War and the first few years of the Commonwealth. George Fox, founder of the Society of Friends, visited Bradford in 1652, just two years after the earliest records we have of the existence of a Quaker sect in Bradford when a Quaker wedding was registered in the town. Quakers and Nonconformists were permitted to keep registers of birth, deaths and marriages separate from the Parish Church Registers, which since the days of Elizabeth I were the only official ones in the town.

The growing Nonconformist population of Bradford is reflected again in the number of Nonconformist churches springing up. As well as the Society of Friends having meeting houses in Bradford, a Society of Baptists is recorded in 1655. In 1662, two years after the Restoration, the Vicar of Bradford, Jonas Waterhouse, was expelled from his living for refusing to conform to the Act of Uniformity, which Charles II introduced to re-establish High Church authority again in the Anglican Church. Bradford's vicar started independent services in his vicarage of a Nonconformist character. Joseph Lister's autobiography also indicates strong groups of Nonconformists at Thornton and Bingley, whose Anglican churchmen sympathised with Wesley's reforms and ideals in the next century.

During the later years of the Commonwealth and Oliver Cromwell's personal rule in Britain, the population in general began to react more and more against Puritanism, especially after the execution of Charles I. When Charles II was restored, the Puritans suffered as a result of this reaction and the Quaker, John Wynn, was bitterly persecuted in Bradford and three times dispossessed for preaching in the town. But, despite this persecution, Bradford, unlike many other townships, remained loyal to its extreme Protestant religion, though a number of Puritans did leave the area to settle in America.

The Act of Uniformity forbade any form of worship except Anglicanism. Neither Roman Catholics nor Nonconformists were allowed to hold office under the Crown, sit in Parliament, or teach in schools. Later, the Nonconformist minister could come not within five miles of a town to preach, which accounts for the little colonies of Nonconformist chapels and meeting houses springing up outside Bradford in villages, such as Thornton, which are now its suburbs.

One result of the Act of Uniformity which affected Bradford men was the Farnley Wood Plot of 1663, which was the conspiracy of a group of West Riding Republicans, many of them ardent Puritans, who wanted 'to restore the rebel Parliament, to reinstate ejected pastors and to remit taxes'. About 300 people gathered in Farnley Woods, near Otley, with the intention of seizing Skipton Castle. Sixteen ringleaders of the plot were Bradford men, including an old Parliamentary officer, John Locock. Twenty-one of the conspirators were executed, but the names of the Bradford plotters are not among them and they probably either fled abroad or withdrew from the plot before its leaders were arrested.

Uniformity brought about the dismissal of Bradford's vicar, Jonas Waterhouse. Another Bradford Puritan was Thomas Sharp, who was minister at Adel Church and brother to Abraham Sharp, the great mathematician. He was compelled to resign his living in the Anglican church and afterwards licensed a room in his father's house at Little Horton to preach in. Two other Bradford Puritans were also ejected from their livings in 1665: Robert Town at Haworth and Joseph Dawson at Thornton. The Presbyterian congregations around Bradford, such as the one Joseph Lister belonged to, eventually became Unitarians or joined other Nonconformist groups such as the Baptists.

In 1685 Charles II died and was succeeded by his brother, James II, a staunch Roman Catholic. At first popular, James II soon lost his popularity by once more trying to force the issue of state religion with his subjects. He made a Roman Catholic a Governor of Ireland, put Catholics in office in the army, and on a more local level, made Catholics Justices of the Peace, men who exercised tremendous power in their regions during the seventeenth and eighteenth centuries. A Roman Catholic, Lord Thomas Howard, was also made Lord Lieutenant of Yorkshire. One important act James II put into operation was his Declaration of Indulgence, which gave freedom of worship to all religious sects, and Bradford's Nonconformists were quick to take advantage of it, though it was designed to help Roman Catholic congregations. A chapel for dissenters was established at Little Horton in 1688 and Heaton Baptist preaching house was registered after the Toleration Act of 1689, when William of Orange and his wife Mary, the Protestant daughter of James II, were on the throne. Two years later further Nonconformist preaching houses were registered at Little Horton and Bowling, and in 1698 Bradford's first Quaker Meeting House was built in Wakefield Road. All these indicate the strong dissenting nature of Bradford religion and the comparative lack of support for the Anglican Church, which did not have a second church in the city till well into the nineteenth century.

One result of Bradford's violent history in the seventeenth century was the decrease in its population and consequent setback in industrial growth. The terrible plague of 1665, which swept the entire country, also took its toll on Bradford citizens when the infection was introduced into the town in a bundle of old clothes from London. By the mid-eighteenth century, the population had still barely reached the size it was a hundred years earlier as the following table from the Parish Registers demonstrates:

	Baptisms	Marriages	Deaths
1639:	209	61	183
1659:	113	38	117
1739:	182	94	134

chapter four

Bradford Comes of Age: The Eighteenth Century

The eighteenth century in Bradford was the prelude to the great economic and social upheaval that swept through the Midlands and North of England in the Industrial Revolution. It was a revolution which changed English society from being a predominantly agricultural and rural one to an industrialized urban society. Cities and towns mushroomed everywhere, often to the detriment of the area they were spawned in and of the people living in them.

The face of the West Yorkshire was changed completely as workers from the counties further south and from Ireland flooded into the fast-growing textile towns. Bradford was changed from a township of textile craftsmen, pursuing their various trades within their own homes and cottages, to a city of dirty factories and slum terraces by the mid-nineteenth century. The Industrial Revolution, gathering momentum throughout the eighteenth century, altered the West Riding from a moorland waste, pitted here and there with odd pockets of industry and smallholding farms, to a complex and highly organised industrial community with over three quarters of Yorkshire's population depending for their living on its industries.

'The South Prospect of Bradford'. The oldest view of Bradford, 1718-19, by Samuel Beck for John Warburton. (Bradford Libraries)

Yorkshire as a whole was an isolated and backward part of the country in the early 1700s. Law and order was administrated by local property-owners, who often had great power. Visiting writers, such as Daniel Defoe and Thomas Gray, spoke disparagingly of the county; Defoe described it as a place where people 'scarcely sowed enough corn to feed their poultry'. Roads were few and poor, the better highways being those stretches of Roman road which still existed. It took nine hours to travel from Bradford to York in the reign of George I (1714-27) and four or five days to make the trip to London, made doubly hazardous by the frequent attacks of highwaymen.

From a map of Bradford and Horton, drawn up in about 1722, the rural nature of the township is very apparent. Trout were still to be caught in Bradford Beck and there were green fields stretching away from the cluster of houses around Kirkgate, Ivegate and Westgate to the hamlets of Horton, Manningham and Bowling. In 1700 there would be fewer than 4,000 persons living in the township. They lived in houses built of local stone in narrow little streets climbing steeply up the hillside to the west of what is now the city centre.

The town was roughly T-shaped, the vertical stem being Kirkgate, which ran from the valley bottom and climbed the hill to meet Ivegate and Westgate. Ivegate fell away to the left down to a bridge over Bradford Beck. Westgate continued to the right climbing towards Silsbridge Lane where there was open country. Across the Beck from Kirkgate, on the top of Church Bank, was the Parish Church and a few houses up Leeds Road. Over the bridge from Ivegate, the road forked; the right-hand fork leading to Little Horton, which housed the residences of some leading Bradford families; the left-hand fork leading to the Wakefield road, a little way up which was a small colony of houses called Goodmansend. Hall Ings were still the meadows they had been since Anglo-Norse times.

below left Warburton's map of Yorkshire, 1720. (Bradford Libraries)

below right Map of the Lordship of Horton, 1722. (Bradford Libraries)

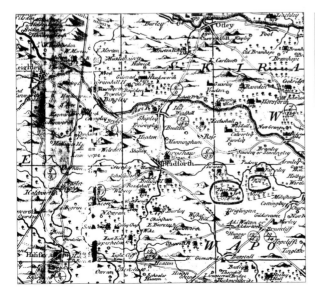

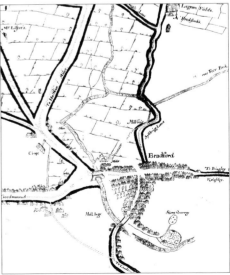

When William and Mary ascended the throne in 1689 a new era started in Bradford's textile industry. The manufacture of woollen goods, for which the town had been renowned since Medieval days, had steadily declined since the civil wars. The textile manufacturers therefore turned their skills to the making of worsted goods which were becoming more and more popular. Worsted looms, in fact, became so popular in the Bradford hand-loom weavers' cottages that there were not sufficient yarn-makers in the town, whose supply had to be supplemented by supplies from villages in Craven. Bradford manufacturers regularly made long journeys each week to the Dales' villages taking out wool to be spun and bringing back finished yarn.

Coal-mining was also becoming a thriving industry and it was the ready accessibility of coal which enabled power-looms to develop at the end of the century. The early pits would be bell-pits and open cast workings. Coal pits were very extensive throughout Bradford and already by 1722 there were many of these pits around Horton. By the mid-nineteenth century pits had spread as far as Manningham and Moorhead (Shipley). Coal was also mined at Bowling and Wyke Moor.

Despite these industrial advances in the eighteenth century, Bradford's growth of population, compared with Halifax and Leeds, was slow. Leeds in the mid-eighteenth century had a population of just under 7,000; in 1801 it had grown to 53,000. Bradford in 1743 had about 4,000 people living in it; by 1801 the four townships of Bradford, Horton, Bowling and Manningham had 13,624 people living in them, Bradford's share being only 6,393. Bradford's phenomenal population growth took place in the next half century.

With the development of better fabrics, newer clothing fashions began to prevail in the eighteenth century. In 1704 new fashions reached England from France, and John Mayhall, in his *Annals of Yorkshire* for 1704, gives us a graphic description of how the well-to-do Bradford citizen would have looked about that time:

New French fashions were adopted by courtiers, physicians and other professional persons in England, also the higher order of gentry, and continued during the reigns of George I and II. This dress of the old English gentleman, as it afterwards came to be called, consisted of a periwig in formal curls, partly contained in a silk bag on the shoulder, a small cocked hat, full-bottomed coat, short breeches, blue or scarlet stockings drawn over the knee, and square-toed shoes, with small buckles and high red heels. Coats were made of velvet, silk or satin, as well as broad cloth, and their colours were very fanciful.

The female attire of the eighteenth century was formal and tasteless. The most odious part of attire introduced in the early part of the century was the large whalebone petticoat, which degenerated into the hooped petticoat, and made a lady to appear as if standing in an inverted tub. In the reigns of George I and II, straw bonnets, loose gowns called sacques, hooded silk cloaks, small muffs and ornamental aprons were worn, with the watch, necklace and the fan, which was sometimes from twelve to eighteen inches in length and beautifully made. Spanish broad-cloth, trimmed with gold lace, was used for ladies' dresses, and fur-bellowed scarfs [sic] were worn from duchess to peasant.

Perhaps the most noticeable institution of Bradford which grew in the eighteenth century was the number of its Nonconformist chapels and sects. Bradford had long been a radical town and in the eighteenth century the independently minded weavers and textile workers, still hand-craftsmen and not machine-minders, quickly adopted the new religions which broke away from the established church.

Baptists founded meeting houses in 1707 at Heaton, where a chapel was built by 1711, and in 1717 the Upper Chapel, Idle, was opened as the first Congregational church in the Bradford area. In 1719 the Presbyterians in Bradford split up; part of the community moving from their headquarters at Little Horton to Chapel Lane, to a site near the Town Hall Square, where a new chapel was built for them which was later occupied by the Unitarians.

Meanwhile, the Parish Church continued to play a leading part too in the lives of the townsfolk. One of its principal roles was in the field of education, in which the vicars and curates of the church played a prominent part as schoolmasters at Bradford Grammar School. The school had grown in size and importance after 1663 when a charter of incorporation had been granted by the newly restored Charles II. In fact, the new title of the school under the terms of the charter was: The Free Grammar School of King Charles the Second at Bradford. The original grammar school building at this time stood near the Parish Church until 1820, when the school moved to new premises in School Lane at the top of Manor Row. The vicar used the schoolroom to collect his tithes and dues, which he also collected at Haworth, the curate of whose church in the seventeenth and eighteenth centuries was appointed by the Vicar of Bradford.

Lessons at the grammar school in those days began early and ended late. One pupil, Thomas Wright, living at Birkenshaw, was to write later:

> At this school they taught every day in the week; began every morning at seven o'clock, and closed every evening at five except Wednesdays and Saturdays, the afternoons of which were devoted to writing, and we lay by at three o'clock. This was the practice summer and winter, so that living a mile off, I had to go and return morning and evening, during every winter season, in the dark.

In 1720 school fees were two guineas a year, and the pupils' board cost £8. Sports at the school then in vogue were marbles, football, tops, kites, shuttlecocks, sliding, skating – and bowls!

In the early eighteenth century, as far as we know, there were no factories in Bradford. Bradford's weavers were home-workers, producing their cloth in their own cottages which often had extra rows of mullion windows built into the upper rooms to allow more light in. Some of these cottages can still be found. Wool-combers banded together in gangs to carry out their craft

and sometimes worked in a separate shed or cottage under the direction of a substantial employer. In fact, unlike other textile centres at the time, such as those in Norwich or the West Country, the great representative figure of the Bradford woollen trade was not the rich merchant clothier, but the small master-craftsman, working himself and employing one or two fellow craftsmen under his own roof. Yorkshire, and Bradford, textile manufacturers sprung up about this time wherever a beck gave plenty of water for washing and bleaching, and, later, for water-power. Quite often the industry's place of origin was the outbuilding of a farmhouse and the typical West Riding employer remained at least one part farmer till late on in the century. For example, Jeremiah Ambler, a Bradford sheep breeder, started his weaving business in a disused barn as late as 1789.

The Bradford worsted manufacturer was nourished by the government throughout the early part of the eighteenth century. Prohibitive duties were imposed on foreign cloth, the import and production of cottons was repressed, and the manufacture of cloth in the colonies was frowned upon. Between 1709 and 1784 Parliament also passed eleven laws to regulate the making and makers of Yorkshire woollen goods and West Riding cloth production increased sixfold during this period; Bradford's worsted trade becoming firmly established and took the lead over its rivals in East Anglia, where worsted production first started in the village of Worsted in the seventeenth century.

As the factory system began to take shape in the early eighteenth century, the various craftsmen ceased to be independent self-employed workmen and became members of gangs or groups of workpeople employed collectively by an enterprising master-craftsman, the forerunner of the mill-owner. The weavers

The Old Market Hall, Bank Street. (Scruton *Pen and Pencil Pictures of Old Bradford*)

and wool-combers began to form themselves into kinds of unions. Often this led to disputes, and to protect the industry an Act of Parliament was passed in 1726 forbidding such combinations, as the early unions were called. However, in 1741 the National Union of Hand Woolcombers was formed in defiance of the Act, calling itself not a combination, but a sick-club. It laid down rules for wage rates, demanded that nobody should employ a comber who was not in the club and declared that 'any man who failed to comply with the rules would be beaten and have his pots broken'. (The pots were vessels which held the combs and kept them warm for combing.) Members were promised that if they came into any trouble, they could travel about the country and be 'carressed' [*sic*] by each club they visited.

True to its early reputation for radicalism, Bradford had some of the first Wesleyan chapels in the country, the first Wesleyan society being formed in 1747. Three years earlier a nonconformist preacher, John Nelson, who was a stonemason from Birstall, had been press-ganged into the army. It was his bold advocacy of Wesley, a personal friend, which brought him into conflict with the Vicar of Birstall who tried to get him out of the way by having him press-ganged into the army, then recruiting for its Jacobite campaign in 1745. He was seized by the press-gang while actually preaching at Adwalton and sent before a tribunal at Halifax, who enlisted him in the army and had him imprisoned in a dungeon. Later, through the intercession of the Countess of Huntingdon, Nelson was released and returned to Bradford to found Wesleyan Methodism in earnest there.

John Wesley himself made frequent visits to Bradford and district. His first visit was made shortly after Nelson's arrest in the summer of 1744 when he preached at Little Horton. Later, when they had an established congregation in Bradford, the Methodists took over a gambling hall called the Bradford Cockpit in 1756. It was here Wesley preached on his subsequent visits to Bradford and where the Revd William Grimshaw, the curate of Haworth Parish Church for twenty years, also preached, supporting Wesley and the principles he stood for.

Bolling Hall. (Scruton Pen and Pencil Pictures of Old Bradford)

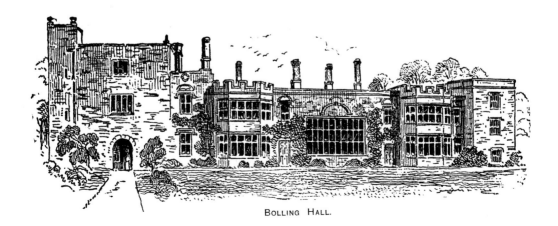

BOLLING HALL.

This building was situated in the Turls (now Tyrrel Street) but it had a large open green in front of it onto which the congregation overflowed when the meeting room was full where Wesley was preaching.

The Cockpit building also housed at various times the Westgate Baptists, the Swedenborgians, a Quaker group, and the followers of two Bradford eccentrics: Joanna Southcott, a woman who imagined herself a prophetess, and 'Prophet' John Wroe of Bradford, who in 1824 tried to walk the Aire dryshod, predicting before a crowd of 30,000 the waters would divide for him to walk across. They didn't! The old Cockpit building had an equally varied life in the secular uses it was put to, for as well as being an eighteenth-century gambling den, it was also used as a temporary barracks, a court-house, a doss-house, a schoolroom, a joiner's shop and finally a warehouse, before it was pulled down well into the nineteenth century.

The late eighteenth century was one of the most enterprising periods of Bradford's history. It had a very energetic and far-seeing group of businessmen in its population, eminent among whom was a group of Quaker merchants, including Benjamin Bartlett, John Hustler, William Wilson and William Maud. All of these men were renowned in their own day for their vigorous campaigning on social issues such as the slave trade and Sunday schools, and in many ways they and their contemporaries laid down the foundation of Bradford's present status as an important industrial city. Typical products of their endeavours were the opening of the first bank in Bradford (in 1760), the Piece Hall for the display of cloth (1773) and the establishment of a subscription library and literary society (1774).

This first known Bradford library of 1774 was a private subscription library whose members paid an entrance fee of one guinea and an annual subscription of five shillings, quite considerable sums for those days. The first treasurer was the Unitarian Minister the Revd John Dean and the first librarian was John

Manor Hall, Kirkgate. (Scruton *Pen and Pencil Pictures of Old Bradford*. Bradford Libraries)

Whitaker, whose salary was £5 a year. Purchases of books are often oddly mixed in with other items in the treasurer's accounts, as the following extract shows:

To	Cicero on Old Age — Calf	5s	—
	The Hermit of Warkworth	2s	6d
	Fire and Candles	7s	—
	Three Weeks After Marriage	5s	—
	An Ounce of Wafers		1½d
	The Silent Woman	4s	6d
	30 quills and a pencil		3d
	Coal and Candles at four Committees	4s	—

Turnpikes

Saturday 9th Feby. 1799
The Roads are entirely blocked up by the Snow – I never remember seeing so much Snow upon the Ground at one time.
    After Breakfast I set off [from Keighley]. We were obliged to flee for the Fields – and had the Walls and the Hedges to pull down – Mr Willm Whitaker lives in

The Bradford portion from the map of the West Riding by Jeffries, 1775. The turnpikes at Clayton, Manningham, Bradford Moor and Wisket Hill are shown.

the Neighbourhood, and kindly lent me his Assistance, and directed us over the
Fields – With Great difficulties – and sometimes on Horseback and sometimes off
– fighting thro' the Snow – in four Hours I reached Bradfd – 10 Miles – I dined at
the Sun – and reached home [Kirkstall] before dark, and very much fatigued.
(From *The Diary of Thomas Butler of Kirstall Forge, Yorkshire, 1796-1799*; edited by
A.E. Butler *et al*, London, 1906.)

Thomas Butler, son of John Butler, of Butler House, Baildon, and proprietor
of Kirkstall Forge in Leeds, spent much of his time travelling around northern
England seeking commissions and meeting clients. Clearly he had the use of a
horse, as would most well-to-do people before the advent of the steam engine
and the motor car. The majority of people, though, walked. It is difficult, now,
to understand life before modern transport. One's world was limited, in large
measure, to the vicinity of home and place of work (often the same) and as far
as one could walk (and then only after a long day's labour and without the boon
of street lighting and concrete pavements).

Traffic on medieval roads was heavy: goods were transported by wagon to and
from ports such as Selby and Liverpool, or to the towns of Halifax, Pontefract,
York or Lancaster. Less bulky items were carried by pack animals and there
was much foot traffic. The roads were maintained by landowners, the Church,
abbeys and by charitable gifts. The principal routes appear to have been good but
lesser roads were often undefined and nothing more than trackways, frequently
impassable in bad weather. It is worth remembering, too, that townships and
villages were small, with large distances of open countryside between them.
Bradford's northern edge was present-day John Street, and there would be a mile
or so of grazing land before reaching the village of Manningham.

Following the dissolution of the monasteries in Henry VIII's reign road
conditions deteriorated and the legal responsibility for their maintenance was
placed on each parish. This led to an erratic situation where some roads were
well looked after in parts but many others remained little more than muddy
tracks. As the country became more mercantile in the seventeenth century it
was recognised that drastic improvements in road transport were needed if
trade was to be encouraged to grow. The stagecoach was already an established
means of travel but it was unsprung, slow and subject to the vicissitudes of
appalling roads and highwaymen. In 1663 an Act of Parliament was passed,
against much opposition, for improving part of the Great North Road and
making users pay for its upkeep. By the early eighteenth century this was seen
as the viable way of creating and maintaining good roads, so many private Acts
of Parliament were passed to allow stretches of road to be made in this way.
Tolls were levied on road users. These were collected at bars or gates set up
at each end of the road and on the side roads linked with the improved road.
These became known as turnpikes, i.e. pikes (bars) that could be turned to allow
vehicles to pass on payment of the appropriate toll.

Unlike Leeds and Wakefield which were on navigable waterways that linked
them to the Ouse, Trent, Don and Humber rivers, and the coastal sea routes

to London and the North Sea ports, Bradford was dependent on roads, many of them hilly. In the preamble to the Leeds-Halifax Turnpike Act of 1740, local roads 'by reason of many heavy carriages passing the same, have become so deep and ruinous, that in Winter and rainy seasons, many parts thereof are impassable for wagons, carts and other wheeled carriages, and very dangerous for travellers…' Bradford got its first turnpike in 1734 running from Leeds to Halifax via Great Horton and Bradford, to which several branches were added. By 1755 turnpike roads linked Bradford to its neighbours Leeds, Halifax, Wakefield, Harrogate, Shipley and Keighley. Shelf, Thornton, Wibsey, Brighouse and Huddersfield were joined later. At each of the toll gates, travellers and goods were charged as they passed into the next gated section. The radial pattern of roads thus established is basically the same that remains today, with the outer ring of toll bars foreshadowing today's ring roads. Although not all the turnpike roads were immediately successful, they were an improvement to the local transport system.

The Turnpike Acts were each promoted by interested, well-off local landowners and merchants who sought to improve the commercial and economic prospects of the area by better transport. These men invested capital to pay for the private parliamentary Act which would give them authority to build the road. The trustees named in the Leeds-Halifax Trust Act of 1740 included three peers, twelve knights, twelve clergy, sixty 'gentlemen' and twenty-three merchants. They had to state the direction of the principal route (usually connecting two or more towns) and give details of any branch roads serving it. They obtained returns on their invested money as interest (typically between $3\frac{1}{2}$% and 5%) charged against the tolls levied. The toll money was used mainly to pay salaries and to provide funds for the upkeep of the road. The charges on the road users were levied in accordance with a tariff laid down in the Act, sometimes levied on the vehicle but more usually on each animal drawing a cart, wagon or carriage, so the more animals, the higher the charge.

Charges varied from Trust to Trust, and on the Leeds-Halifax Trust the charges were:

Five horses or more – 9d

Four horses – 6d

Two or three horse – 4d

One horse – 3d

Every extra draught horse – $\frac{1}{2}$d

Every drove of oxen, etc. – 6d per score

Calves, hogs – $2\frac{1}{2}$d per score

There were exemptions for churchgoers, vehicles carrying farm produce and people voting in parliamentary elections.

Those who collected the tolls were known as toll-gate keepers and lived in purpose-built cottages strategically sited along the roads. Most tollhouses had angled fronts with windows giving views up and down the road. Between these

The toll bar at Spinkwell (Bolton Road). Drawing by William Scuton. (Bradford Libraries)

was a door which gave access directly to the gate across the road. The toll-gate keepers were first employed directly by the trustees of the turnpike but it was later found more economic to rent the tolls to the highest bidder, usually on an annual lease.

These new roads were not universally popular. Local historian James notes:

> About this time (1745), commodious roads began to be formed in these parts, in place of the narrow packhorse lanes. The turnpikes were, by the lower class, universally regarded as an obnoxious regulation, more adopted for the convenience of the wealthy portion of the community, whose carriages could hardly pass on the old roads, than the benefit of such class.

Most of the early turnpikes were aligned along existing routes with some small adjustments for bends and gradients. The quality of the surfaces was generally improved by laying graded gravel and stone and improving drainage. New bridges were sometimes built to take the road or old bridges widened. Some of these remain today. Milestones were set up along the route to give distances between the principal towns. The improved transport generated by the turnpike system required elaborate serving and coaching inns, many already long established, and they were to play a crucial role. The inns built alongside the roads had large backyards with stables for the horses. The inns provided a change of horses as well as food and accommodation for the travellers. Horses were provided by the proprietors of the coaches.

The coaches were gradually improved and the Royal Mail coaches (started in 1784) became the luxury transport of their day. For the first time letters written by the general public could be transmitted reliably and regularly – a development of great significance in those pre-telephone days. In the late eighteenth and early nineteenth centuries a letter from London General Post Office would be

Union Passage and Post Office.
(Bradford Libraries)

delivered in Bradford within twenty-four hours. Letters and packages would be delivered to the nearest inn. Royal Mail coaches on well-surfaced turnpike roads were reaching speeds of 8mph in the late eighteenth century increasing to 10mph in the early years of Queen Victoria. The journey from Leeds to London which took four days in 1760, took only twenty-four hours in 1838.

SOME OF THE COACHES THAT SERVED BRADFORD

Alexander (1820-43) Leeds – Bradford – Bingley – Keighley – Skipton
   (1820-23) Bradford – Halifax

Britannia (1818-21) Leeds – Bradford – Bingley – Keighley – Skipton

Commerce (1828-40) Leeds – Bradford – Halifax – Manchester

Courier (1833-42) Leeds – Bradford – Halifax

Defence (1824-34) Leeds & Bradford market coach

Diligence (1789-91) Leeds – Bradford – Bingley – Keighley – Settle – Kirkby
   Lonsdale – Kendal

Duke of Leeds (1828-39) Leeds – Bradford – Halifax – Manchester

Highflyer. York – Leeds – Bradford – Halifax – Manchester – Liverpool

Invincible (1824-42) Leeds – Bradford – Bingley – Keighley – Colne – Burnley
   – Blackburn – Preston

Mail (1822-42) Leeds – Bradford – Halifax – Rochdale – Manchester

Mail (1841-45) Leeds – Bradford – Bingley – Keighley – Skipton – Settle
   – Lancaster

Neptune (1813–20) Leeds – Bradford – Halifax – Rochdale – Preston – Liverpool

Rockingham (1836-40) Bradford – Leeds – London

Trafalgar (1807-34) Hull – Leeds – Bradford – Manchester

Traveller (1826-43) Leeds – Bradford

Union (1822-35) Leeds – Bradford

(Source: Tom Bradley, *The Old Coaching Days in Yorkshire*)

Each company used a particular coaching inn. The London-bound *Rockingham*, for example, started from the Bowling Green Inn at 7.00 a.m. to connect with the London coach at the Golden Lion in Leeds, which left at 8.30 a.m. (After April 1836, the *Rockingham* ran through to London from Bradford without a change of coach.) In 1838, some thirteen coaches left Leeds for Bradford, the first at 6.30 a.m. and the last at 8.00 p.m.

Canals

The determination with which John Hustler pursued the idea, and eventual construction of, the Leeds & Liverpool Canal, with its branch canal to Bradford, is typical of the man and his age in Bradford's history and worth commenting on in more detail. The initial idea of a Leeds-Liverpool canal probably came from Longbottom, a pupil of John Smeaton, the Leeds engineer, and a notice was inserted in the county newspaper *The York Courant* on 7 August 1764: 'As the Rivers Aire and Ribble may be so easily joined at different places and rendered navigable between Leeds and Preston, at an expense which gentlemen who have estates on the banks may readily supply, it is thought proper to mention it to the public at this juncture'. John Hustler was the guiding light behind the

The Bowling Green Hotel, from which many a stagecoach would depart. (Rhodes, *Bradford Past and Present*, p.39. Courtesy Bradford Libraries)

new venture which was to encurage industry, not only in Bradford, as Hustler knew it would, but for much of the North of England whose emerging towns and cities were connected by it.

In 1766 the first general meeting of parties interested in the proposed Leeds-Liverpool Canal was held in Bradford, at the Sun Inn. Bradford was to remain the headquarters of the canal company well into the nineteenth century, for the head office was there until 1850 and the company's bankers and solicitors were Bradford business concerns till much later. Of the capital invested in the new company, much came from Bradford, too; London bankers alone subscribing more than Bradford's businessmen.

By 1770 Parliament had passed the necessary legislation enabling work to begin on the canal, and seven years later, in 1777, the canal was open for traffic between Leeds, Shipley and Skipton. Bradford's link canal, remembered now by Canal Road which follows its route, was built by 1774. It was 3 miles long, 5 feet deep and fell 86 feet by locks from Bradford to the junction at Shipley. Industry and commerce as a whole benefited tremendously and it was not until over seventy years later that better commercial links between West Riding centres of industry were established with the creation of a new railway network. The new canal, which was Hustler's 'brainchild', meant that coal could be transported more quickly and in greater bulk to the growing textile towns such as Keighley, Shipley and Bingley. Barges on the return run were able to bring massive supplies of limestone down from Skipton and the Craven lime quarries, to be used in a wide variety of ways; in the building industry, in the Bowling Ironworks, and also in agriculture.

John Hustler's part in the development of Bradford did not end with the lead he gave in the construction of the Leeds & Liverpool Canal, which was eventually completed in 1815. He helped form the Worsted Committee to protect the domestic worsted manufacturers against embezzlement by their commission out-weavers, the unscrupulous of whom stole wool freely. Hustler was the

Old Ivegate. (Scruton *Pen and Pencil Pictures of Old Bradford*)

Worsted Committee's first chairman and he later gave evidence on behalf of the committee before a Parliamentary Committee investigating the export of British wools. He was also instrumental in the building of Bradford's Piece Hall in 1773 which did so much to attract trade to Bradford's textile industry. The first Piece Hall, built by textile trade subscribers, was used primarily for the display and marketing of cloth, which previously had had to be shown either in the homes of the manufacturers or in public houses. The Piece Hall also served a variety of other purposes, including a courthouse and concert hall. The first known public performance of Handel's *Messiah* in Bradford was given there in 1774.

There seems something significant that, despite these very important industrial developments in Bradford during this period of dynamic enterprise of the 1770s, the town still remained essentially rural. It was still a very attractive market town with curious folk customs such as the festivals in honour of the textile industry's patron saint, Bishop Blaize, the legendary inventor of wool-combing. The notorious position that Bradford came to hold for filth and squalor, in common with other cities spawned in the Industrial Revolution, was not realised until the nineteenth century was well advanced. Bradford had only one solitary new mill chimney as late as 1800 and trout still swam in its beck.

The local historian, William Scruton, describes Bradford as he himself remembered it described by older inhabitants who lived there at the end of the eighteenth century:

The town proper consisted of a cluster of buildings in the neighbourhoods of Kirkgate, Westgate, the Turls [Tyrrel Street], Bridge Street and New Street [Market Street]; and from this centre, straggling and irregular lines of buildings, chiefly houses, stretched out in the direction of Good-mans-end, Barker-end and Westgate. Beyond, all was open countryside, pleasantly diversified by trees and hedgerows (in modern times replaced by ugly walls), waving cornfields, and here and there the quaint old homesteads or mansions of a race of gentry long since departed … The well-to-do people had their houses in Kirkgate, Westgate, the neighbourhood of the parish church and at 'Town-end'. The last-named place was a cluster of good residences reaching from Chapel Lane to the bottom of Horton Road … In the space between Kirkgate and the front of the Bowling Green Hotel (at the bottom of Tyrrell Street) a rookery flourished, and in Hall Ings there was a fine plantation of trees … There were only two roads by which to get to Manningham; one by way of Skinner Lane (Cheapside) and the other by Westgate and Northgate (then known as Fair-Gap). Manningham Lane lay between hedges, and was so narrow that Mr. E.C. Lister (who lived at Manningham Hall) found it difficult to get along it with his carriage and usually preferred driving round by Whetley Hill and Westgate … At the close of the century, the town had no other protection than what a half dozen watchmen could give. The streets had no better light than what a few dismal oil lamps could impart, which, with an eye to economy, were placed at considerable distances apart. That time-honoured functionary, the Parish Beadle, was still an important personage in Bradford, notwithstanding that his services were but poorly remunerated, for his stipend only amounted to four pounds and one suit of clothes per annum.

1 N.S. Crichton. Miryshay, Barkerend, *c*. 1875. (Bradford Museums and Galleries)

2 N.S. Crichton. Old Paper Hall, High Street, Barkerend, *c*. 1875. (Bradford Museums and Galleries)

3 S. Crichton. View in High Street, *c*. 1875. (Bradford Museums and Galleries)

4 N.S. Crichton. Parish
Church, North Side, *c.* 1875.
(Bradford Museums and
Galleries)

5 N.S. Crichton. Back View,
Church Steps Inn, *c.* 1875.
(Bradford Museums and
Galleries)

6 Sim Ward. Old Inn, undated. (Bradford Museums and Galleries)

7 H.T. Winn. Old Toll Bar House, *c*. 1898. (Bradford Museums and Galleries)

8 View of Bradford by Wilson Anderton, *c.* 1850.(Bradford Museums and Galleries)

9 View of Bradford by William Cowen, 1849. (Bradford Museums and Galleries)

10 One of the many magnificent stone buildings of the Little Germany mercantile quarter.

11 The Post Office building in Forster Square. One of the many fine buildings that survive.

12 The Wool Exchange (detail).

13 above The University of Bradford building, 1966.

14 right Ivegate.

15 The Wool Exchange.

Two reasons for the late appearance of factories in Bradford may have been the lack of force in Bradford Beck to drive water-powered looms and also the hostility of the textile operatives to mechanised power of any sort. Water-driven spinning frames were working in many other areas near Bradford long before they made their appearance in Bradford itself. The first mechanised water-powered spinning frame in the West Riding was built at Addingham in 1787, and shortly afterwards others were operated at Leeming, near Oxenhope, and Ilkley. Bradford in the 1790s still spun yarn on spinning mules turned by hand and on machinery driven by a horse gin. The 1790s were also years of depression in Bradford's textile trade; years when few manufacturers would risk capital in new machinery.

In 1793 the first attempt to establish a steam-powered spinning mill in Bradford was thwarted by Luddite violence and in the same year a Mr Buckley, who wanted to build a steam-powered cotton mill, was threatened with legal action by the town's leading inhabitants on the grounds that his mill chimney would be a public nuisance. He eventually built his mill in Todmorden! Bradford's first steam-powered mill-owner had to use his fists to establish his concern in 1799, when he fought his way onto the building site one day. After this display of muscle-power on the part of the manufacturer, Bradford accepted steam-power and the town was launched into its period of rapid growth, having, as it did, abundant coal supplies within its boundaries being worked by several well-established collieries in the Low Moor area. The Bowling and Low Moor Iron Companies, founded in 1788 and 1791, were also firmly established and ready to play an important part in the development of Bradford's steam mills by their ready supply of boilers, steam engines and ironwork.

In his *Annals of Yorkshire*, John Mayhall, the nineteenth-century diarist and antiquarian, records:

> The ironworks in the neighbourhood of Bradford are universally known. The manor of Royds Hall, together with minerals under the estate, was purchased from the last proprietor in 1788, by the ancestors of Messrs Hird, Dawson and Hardy, who originally established the celebrated Low Moor Iron and Coal Works, now the most important in the north of England. The works comprise furnaces, forges, tilts and mills, on a very extensive scale, both for the manufacture of pig and bar iron, and for rolling and slitting it into sheets, bars and rods, with foundries for the casting of cannon and ordnance of all kinds, in which several steam engines of great power are also employed. In addition to these, boilers for steam engines, sugar pans for the East and West Indies, water pipes of large calibre, and castings of every kind are manufactured, in which more than 2,000 persons are employed day and night. The Bierley Ironworks were commenced in 1810 by Henry Leah and James Marshall. These works, conducted on an extensive scale, are confined solely to the manufacture of pig-iron, which, being the produce of ore from the same mine, is equal in quality with that of the Low Moor. At Bowling, the substratum abounds with coal and iron ore, which have been wrought for half a century by the Bowling Iron Company, whose works are very extensive. The accumulated heaps of refuse from the mines, forming huge mounds surrounding the excavations, have been planted with trees, which adds greatly to the aspect of the neighbourhood.

Bradford's first workhouse in Barkerend Road. It was built in 1738 and used until a Poor Law Institution was built in 1851. (Bradford Libraries)

Mayhall also has another important comment to make on the industry which launched Bradford into the nineteenth and twentieth centuries as a city of world renown. He spotlights the rapid growth of the worsted industry at the end of the eighteenth century, an industry which was to transform Bradford from a little market town supported by home industries such as handloom weaving and wool-combing, much of which was carried on by part-time farmers, to the vast sprawling city of back-to-back houses and to dirty mills it became notorious for by the mid-nineteenth century. Mayhall writes:

> The demand in foreign markets, from the year 1782 to 1792, for English worsted goods, greatly exceeded that of any former period; but after the breaking out of the French war, the worsted trade at Halifax began to decline.
>
> About this time the spinning of worsted by machinery was established at Bradford and the vicinity; and, continuing to increase, drew round that place the manufacturers of worsted goods on the decline of the Halifax trace. Bradford is now the principal seat of the worsted manufacture in Yorkshire; and some of the proprietors of the worsted mills, besides supplying the smaller manufacturers with yarn, employ a very great number of looms themselves, and carry on this branch of trade on a scale of extent never before known in the worsted manufacture.
>
> The worsted manufactory has been the means of increasing the prosperity and population of the town of Bradford, in a manner altogether unprecedented in British history. It now presents an astonishing scene of active and successful industry; its market is one of the greatest in the kingdom, and its manufacturers and merchants are distinguished by their skill, diligence and enterprise. The Piece Hall, at Bradford, is a tolerably commodious mart for stuffed goods; it is one hundred and forty-four feet long by thirty-six broad, and is divided into two apartments — the upper and the lower chamber.

chapter five

From Town to Borough: Bradford 1800-1847

Bradford's population in 1801 was 13,264. (Bradford is defined as the area that was to become the Borough of Bradford in 1847, i.e. the townships of Bradford, Bowling, Horton and Manningham.) The town was the twenty-fifth largest provincial town in England, coming after Shrewsbury, which had 14,739 inhabitants. Fifty years later, Bradford's population had increased phenomenally to 103,778 and it was the ninth largest city in England. After Middlesborough, Bradford expanded the quickest of any English provincial town in the first half of the nineteenth century and the figures below give some indication of the size and acceleration of this phenomenal growth from 1801, the date of the first national census:

1801   13,264   (Bradford, Horton, Bowling and Manningham)
1811   16,012
1821   26,309
1831   43,527
1841   66,715
1851   103,778
1861   106,218
1871   145,827
1881   183,032 (Plus Bolton)
1891   216,361 (As 1881 plus Allerton, Heaton, Thornbury and part of Tyersal)
1901   279,767 (As 1891 plus North Bierley, Tong, Thornton, Eccleshill and Idle)

(As can be seen from this table, the boundaries of the town changed so comparisons are not straightforward.)

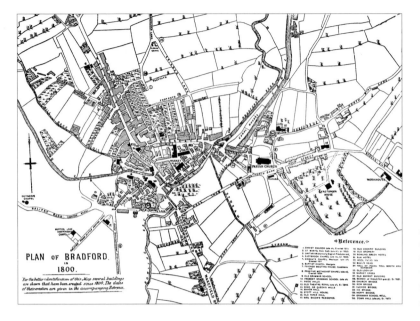

Plan of Bradford, 1800, by Shepherd Brothers. The canal basin, market place, workhouse and mill goit are all to be seen in this fascinating map. (Scruton *Pen and Pencil Pictures of Old Bradford*)

Squalor

With little or no concern for town planning, it is not hard to imagine how Bradford, in common with other northern and midland cities, came to have an unenviable reputation for slums and filth. Even now, Bradford still has many of the slums and shoddy houses which were thrown up during its period of rapid growth. In terms of material wealth, there is no doubt Bradford was at its most prosperous during the nineteenth century. In terms of human misery that century, or at least the first half, was probably also the blackest in the township's history. Yet Bradford was not alone in this. Towns like Leeds, Manchester and Liverpool were all suffering the same fate, as were the smaller growing textile communities like Keighley, Batley and Huddersfield. The semi-rural township of 1800 described by Scruton changed rapidly over the next fifty years. Large numbers of immigrant families, from Ireland and the rural south, changed the character of its population. Their houses and mills covered the surrounding countryside. In 1845 one government official, James Smith, wrote in a parliamentary paper concerning his visit to Bradford:

> The general state of the surface of the streets of Bradford is respectable, but in most of the inferior and cross streets, chiefly inhabited by the working classes, the condition is quite otherwise. Few of those are paved at all; none of them properly. In some streets a piece of paving is laid half across the street, opposite one man's tenement, whilst his opposite neighbour contents himself with a slight covering of soft engine ashes, through which the native clay of the subsoil is seen protruding, with unequal surface, and pools of slop water and filth are visible all over the surface. The dungheaps are found in several parts in the streets, and open privies are seen in many directions. Large swill-tubs are placed in various places by pig-

feeders for collecting the refuse from the families, for which they pay in some cases from 1d to 2d per week.

The chief sewerage, if sewerage it can be called, of the inferior streets and of the courts, is in the open channels, and from the rough and unequal surface of the streets, the flow is tardy and the whole soil is saturated with sewage water. The main sewage is discharged, either into the brook [Bradford Beck] or into the terminus or basin of a canal which runs into the lower part of the town. The water of this basin is often so charged with decaying matter, that in hot weather bubbles of sulphurated hydrogen are continually rising to the surface, and so much is the atmosphere loaded with that gas, that watch-cases and other materials of silver become black in the pockets of the workmen employed near the canal. The stench is sometimes very strong, and fevers prevail much all around. Taking the general condition of Bradford, I am obliged to pronounce it to be the most filthy town I visited.

In 1839/41, Edwin Chadwick, in his Health of Town's Commission Report on Bradford, reported that the average age at death in Bradford was eighteen and one-third years compared with about thirty-four years for Kendal, though much depended on the occupation of the deceased. Thus gentry and professional people in Bradford had a life expectancy of thirty-nine years compared with a wool-comber's sixteen years and a rural farmer's thirty-six.

Why was this terrible transformation allowed to happen to the town and its adjoining villages which had shown such promise under the care of men like Hustler and his contemporaries during the latter part of the eighteenth century? There is no simple answer, but generally speaking the men responsible for the administration and planning of the township were swamped by technological and social forces they could not contain. Sudden economic growth, fed by the natural resources so readily available in the area, prevented their being able to cope with the massive influx of population which had to be housed near the mills and factories they worked in. Bradford Dale became choked with hastily and cheaply built dwellings before any legislation could be passed to curb the unscrupulous builders and land-grabbers of the period. There was also the selfish self-interest of those responsible for this growth: entrepreneurs whose motivation was minimizing costs and maximizing profits. Expressions such as 'hands', 'lower classes' or 'labouring classes' revealed a callous attitude to the workforce which is hard to accept today.

Local government was in the hands of the parish vestry, an outmoded and incompetent body which appointed the township's officials, who were often influenced by the new manufacturers. The manufacturers' prime concern was making money, not caring for the social development of the town and its inhabitants. A local committee appointed by the parish vestry in 1831 to investigate the need for a police force ruefully admitted 'that whilst the population and commerce of the town had rapidly increased, its moral and municipal discipline is on the decline'. Apathy at a national level was even more pronounced, for Bradford, in common with the mushrooming industrial cities throughout the country, had no voice in Parliament, being without a Member there until the Reform Bill was passed in 1832. Consequently, whatever public-spirited element did exist among the new Bradford industrialists, it had little or no power to halt the poor condition the growing township was falling into.

Although the civic development of Leeds was just as chaotic and inadequate as Bradford, Leeds at least did have some public-spirited medical men like doctors Baker and Thackeray, who, early on in the nineteenth century, vigorously condemned the unhygienic and filthy living and working conditions in the city. On the other hand, William Sharp, surgeon at the Dispensary at Bradford, could see little wrong in the conditions of the mills he visited in Bradford; though he had to admit that he considered that children working from six in the morning to seven at night, with half an hour for breakfast and forty minutes for dinner was rather too long a period of work. Thomas Wilson, a doctor living at Bingley, who also inspected mills in the Bradford area, was equally bland in the replies he gave before a parliamentary committee in 1818 set up by the House of Lords. Wilson admitted:

- to have examined 570 people in ten hours in the different factories
- that his examination was cursory and slight
- that he found fifteen children under the age of nine
- that a lad of the age of fifteen years was sufficiently employed if he was kept at work twelve hours out of the twenty-four
- that young persons did not need any recreation or amusement during the day
- that their health would not suffer if they worked seven days a week
- that time for breakfast and dinner should not be included in those twelve hours
- that six in the morning in winter was a reasonable starting time, and half past five in summer
- and that working a ten-year-old child during the night would not damage their health

In 1803 a group of Bradford businessmen, headed by John Hustler, junior, tried to combat the worst excesses of rapid industrial growth, which would have just been making themselves apparent by 1803. Several of these public-spirited men offered to subscribe money to defray the expense of obtaining an Act of Parliament which set up in Bradford a committee called the Lighting and Watching Commissioners. The Act was passed in June 1803 and fifty-eight leading Bradfordians, including John Hustler and John Hardy (whose family took a leading part in nineteenth-century parliamentary affairs in Bradford) became Commissioners.

The Act was termed: 'An Act for paving, lighting, watching and improving the town of Bradford and part of the hamlet of Little Horton, and for removing and preventing all nuisances therein'. Its powers were rigorously curtailed, however, and unfortunately it did not supersede the parish vestry surveyors, who held the real authority in Bradford and who were not ousted from power until the creation of a more democratically elected corporation in 1847. It does reveal, however, that there was a section of Bradford's business community which was genuinely concerned about the indiscriminate building and lack of town-planning which was going on.

Notices calling a meeting of the Commissioners were pinned to the door of the Parish Church or announced by the town-crier and the first meeting was held at the Bull's Head inn on 1 July 1803. The Bull's Head was in Westgate and in front of it was held the town market, with its butter cross, round which the local farmers' wives brought their dairy goods for sale on Thursdays and Saturdays. Nearby was also the pillory at Bradford, used well into the nineteenth century. The Bull's Head seemed a favourite meeting-place for Bradford businessmen in 1803 and was the forerunner of Bradford Chamber of Commerce. The Bradford Club, formed about 1760, had its headquarters at the Bull's Head by the beginning of the nineteenth century.

The Commissioners held many of the powers exercised by the City Council today. Such matters as street-lighting and the provision of water-carts (there was no piped water at this time) fell within their province. One of their duties was to ensure 'that no necessary house [earth closet] or bog house shall be emptied at any other time than between the hours of ten at night and five in the morning'. The Commissioners were also empowered to employ watchmen and to 'provide them with proper arms, ammunition, weapons and clothing for the discharge of their duty, and to erect and set up watch-houses and watch-boxes'. In other words, these early watchmen held many of the responsibilities the modern police force holds. Before 1803 the 'watching' of the town had been done on a voluntary basis and the guarding of the town was carried out by local bands of yeomen volunteers till the establishment of a regular police force.

Still a Market Town

Some idea of the size of Bradford in 1803 is gathered from the information setting out the bounds which the watchmen had to walk round and secure. They were:

> the whole of the old Market Place and Westgate, as far as the house occupied by Mr. Johnson [Silsbridge Lane]; the whole of Kirkgate, the whole of Ivegate, and from Ive-bridge to Mr. Wood's house in Great Horton Lane; as far as Mr. Rand's mill in Little Horton Lane; from Ive-bridge to the Quakers' Meeting House in Goodman's-end; the whole of Chapel Lane; the whole of New Street [Market Street]; the whole of Bank Street, and from the top of Bank Street into Ivegate; the new Market Place [now the Wool Exchange], and from thence through the Piece-Hall Yard into Kirkgate; from the Church Bridge to Stott Hill; from the Church Bridge up to Paper Hall [in Barkerend Road]; and from Westgate into Silsbridge Lane, as far as Mr. Crabtree's house.

The built-up area of Bradford in 1800 measured rather less than half a square mile. It was a tightly drawn, settled area contained mostly in the bend of the Beck where it turns north. There were minor extensions into Horton township along Great Horton Road and Bridge Street, and across the Beck, north of the Parish Church (now the Cathedral). Surrounding this tiny core were strip fields. The large East Brook estate occupied a park just east of the church. The medieval goit (channel) ran as an open watercourse, paralleling the Thornton Turnpike on the north, and to the south the Bradford Beck. A vastly different Bradford, indeed, from the reconstructed centre of the late nineteenth century and today.

Early on the Commissioners prepared a list of houses in their district and levied rates on the township of Bradford and part of the hamlet of Little Horton, which stood some way off the town proper. The names in these early rate books provide an interesting glance at the life of Bradford.

It was still a little market town with the factory system barely having a foothold in the place. The Society of Friends was numerically very strong and many of its members took a leading role in the life of the town. As well as the Hustler family, the Maud family in Westgate were Quakers and William Maud was a doctor with an extensive practice in and around Bradford. He was known by his contemporaries as 'Owd' Billy Maud and was an ardent disciple of Jenner, the discoverer of the Smallpox vaccination, which Dr Maud carried out free of charge to all Bradfordians who requested it. Dr Maud was also a bitter opponent of the slave trade and campaigned vigorously against it.

The houses of the middle class and the manufacturers seemed noticeably more intermingled with the artisans' houses than was to be the case in succeeding years. Although the houses of the well-to-do were grander and greater, they were often next to the houses of craftsmen and workers. In Kirkgate, for example, there were the Hardys living in Manor Hall, at one end

Parish Church (now the Cathedral) and vicarage in 1810. (Scruton *Pen and Pencil Pictures of Old Bradford*)

Bradford Cathedral today.

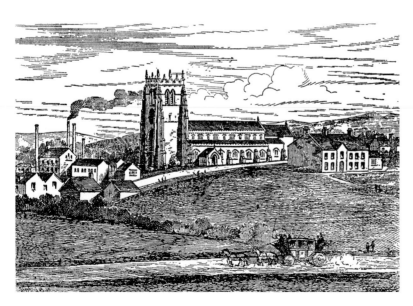

of the social scale (John Hardy was a barrister), and only a little further down the road were the business premises and dwelling places of George Linforth, a woollen draper, John Nicholson, the printer, James Stead, a glazier, and John Hartley, a saddler. Along Kirkgate were also built many of the old coaching inns of the early nineteenth century. There was the Talbot, the Nag's Head, the Royal Oak, the White Lion, the Shoulder of Mutton, the Malt Shovel and the White Horse, all within a very short distance of each other and indicating Bradford's importance both as a market centre and staging town for traffic at the beginning of the century. Neither were these inns the only ones in the centre of the town, for there were another popular set of inns and public houses in New Street, which, as its name suggests, was of comparatively recent erection compared with the older lanes of the town, such as Kirkgate. Next to the Hope and Anchor Inn in New Street there was a saddler called William Brown, whose son, Henry Brown, later became Mayor of Bradford. The widow of William Brown established a business as outfitter on her husband's death, a business which flourished greatly under her acumen. The fondly remembered department store of Brown, Muff & Co. of recent history (the site is on the corner of Market Street and Ivegate) is the direct descendant of Widow Brown's business established in the early years of the last century.

In 1805, what fashionable part of Bradford there may have been was near the Parish Church in Barkerend and in Town-end. The blind Vicar of Bradford, John Crosse, lived at the vicarage in Church Bank, and just below his house, at the bottom of Church Bank, was the old grammar school. On Stott Hill was built the Old Hall, where Joseph Priestley, chief manager of the Leeds & Liverpool Canal Company, lived, and his neighbour was an attorney, John Robert Ogden. The manufacturer, James Garnett, who set up the first spinning machine in Bradford in 1794, also lived in this vicinity at the Paper Hall.

After about 1805 matters seemed to become steadily worse in the town. Clouds of smoke emanated from the blast furnaces of Birkenshaw and Low Moor, and steam engines were beginning to disturb the rural peace. Steam-driven worsted mills started to appear in 1801. The accelerated growth appeared to be too much for the new Commissioners, and the contractors they hired to keep the town clean were inefficient. Eventually the Commissioners turned to the Union Workhouse managers and sought the employment of able-bodied paupers to clean up the streets; but the workhouse managers asked too much for the labour the paupers did and the men were withdrawn, so the streets soon became intolerably filthy.

Old streets and lanes were given new names about this time, too. High Street was called Barkerend and the lane running from Church Bridge to Church Bank was named Well Street. Dead Lane (scene of much bitter hand-to-hand fighting during the siege of Bradford in 1642 when it was said to have received the name Dead Lane) was renamed Vicar Lane. Other streets, formerly only footpaths, to be given names were Bridge Street, Bank Street, Northgate and Balme Gate. Toad Lane was altered to Chapel Lane and New Street was changed to Market Street.

Some effort was made to introduce street-lighting by the Commissioners in 1804, but their efforts were often foiled by vandals breaking what few street lamps there were, which were oil-and-wick lamps at this time. The paucity of available funds also severely hampered their other civic work and the Lord of the Manor, Benjamin Rawson, often opposed many of their efforts at improvement, since it meant his having to pay out more money and his privileges, too, were often encroached upon. The Highway Surveyors held equal authority with the Commissioners, but the Highway Surveyors were often dilatory in carrying out recommendations at town improvement made to them by the Commissioners. Many private individuals also resented the Commissioners ordering them to remove abandoned carts or private property which was causing a public nuisance in the town. One instance where the latter case often obtained was in the Commissioners' attempts to remove pigs from the centre of the town. Many Bradford families owned pigs in the early nineteenth century, and allowed them to wander around the streets scavenging for offal and garbage which had been thrown away and which was plentiful.

The Commissioners tried hard to clear away this nuisance from the streets, but for a long time they were unsuccessful. Finally, because they could not keep the pigs from wandering about during the week, the Commissioners tried appealing to the Sabbatarian respects of the townsfolk and issued the following notice:

> Whosoever shall allow their pigs to run loose in the streets on the Sabbath Day will be prosecuted with the utmost rigour of the law.

Many other private citizens openly flouted the authority of the Commissioners, who grew more and more disheartened with their task of trying to cope with a growing township whose new citizens were not very public-spirited. In 1814, for example, a local tanner, William Whitaker, whose business was in Chapel Lane, continued to wash his skins in the Bradford Beck despite being indicted by the Commissioners. The Commissioners' loss of interest becomes very apparent as time goes on and in 1817 there was no meeting of the Commissioners between 6 January and 29 August, and much of the improvement, such as it was, in Bradford during this time was effected by the Vestry Council. There was little paving or real roadwork carried out by 1821 when the population had risen to 26,209.

Developments

Between 1801 and 1821 a number of important events had taken place which were to affect the future history of the town. In 1803 the first shipment of merino wool from Australia was brought to England by Captain John Macarthur and auctioned in London. Captain Macarthur had introduced merino sheep into Australia for wool production in 1796 and in 1805 he supplemented his flock out there with rams bought from King George's own flock at Windsor. In 1808 the Revd Samuel Marsden of Farsley brought the first samples of Australian wool back from New South Wales, where he had emigrated. In 1810 he returned to Australia and began exporting wholesale wool to Bradford.

Wesleyan Methodism gained much popular support in Bradford at the early part of the century and in 1812 Woodhouse Grove School was opened at Apperley Bridge, initially for the education of sons of Wesleyan ministers. It was here that the Revd Patrick Brontë used to visit a colleague and where he met his wife, Maria Branwell. The Anglican Church, too, acting on a report of the Ecclesiastical Commissioners that Bradford, with a population in 1811 of 16,012, was lacking in churches, built only the second Anglican church there since the founding of the Parish Church. The new church, Christ Church at the top of Darley Street, was started in 1815. (It was demolished in 1879 to make a way through from Darley Street to Manningham Lane.)

In 1816 the entire length of the Leeds-Liverpool Canal was completed, linking Bradford, through its branch canal, with major industrial cities on both sides of the Pennines. The head offices of the canal were situated in Bradford. A new grammar school was built in 1818 to replace the old school buildings near the church, and Bradford's oldest musical institution, the Old Choral Society, was formed as the Bradford Musical Friendly Society in 1821.

The period 1822 to 1847 saw the continued accelerated growth of Bradford and some of its most turbulent times. In its own way, it was an era as violent in civil riots as the period of the Civil War had been. Loom breakers' and Chartists' activities were manifold and, following the end of the Napoleonic Wars in 1815 and the rise in corn prices, poverty and unemployment were rife.

'A map of the Borough of Bradford as determined by the Commissioners (appointed by The Honourable [sic] the Commons House of Parliament, 1834).' Although not as clear as the Shepherds' map above, the rural nature of the surrounding area is clear to see. (Bradford Libraries)

W. Harker, Victoria Mills, Wakefield Road.

Victoria Mills, Wakefield Road. One of the early Victorian mills. (J. Currey, *Illustrated Commercial Guide*, 1858. Courtesy Bradford Libraries)

Industry continued to grow in Bradford during this period and with it a parallel deterioration in living and working conditions. In 1801 there was only one mill in Bradford; by 1841 there were sixty-seven. 'The manufacturers are removing to Bradford as fast as they can get accommodated with looms', ran one comment of the *Bradford Observer* in 1836. A journalist of the same paper, James Burnley, also commenting about the same period, said that there were many parts of Bradford which were 'regarded by dwellers in spacious streets and commodious habitations as forbidden regions ... I wonder how many of the well-dressed, well-fed people, who daily pass up and down Westgate, have really any experience of, or seriously consider, the wretchedness, the misery, and the disease, of which the entrance to Silsbridge Lane is the threshold?'

The Silsbridge area was then notorious for its slums and many of its occupants were Irish immigrants. By 1851 there were almost 10,000 Irish immigrants housed in Bradford, forming nearly a tenth of the city's population. (Silsbridge Lane has since disappeared and its place taken by development in the Grattan Road area.)

The Bradford Beck continued to get worse and was nothing more than an open sewer by 1843. William Whitaker, the tanner called to task in 1814 for washing his skins in the beck, would have had them ruined had he tried to do so thirty years later! The canal, too, was filthy and disease-ridden by the 1840s. Such drains as there were in the town were emptied into the canal basin and this muck was fed by that coming down the Bradford Beck. The manufacturers below the floodgates of the canal drew water from the canal for their mill boilers, and having been used there, it was transported back again through effluents back into the canal so that, as one report said, 'the waters of the canal are scarcely ever cool in summer, and constantly emit the most offensive gases'.

Although some attempt had been made at smoke abatement in 1814, little further action was taken and Bradford became renowned as 'The Black City'.

The canal was nicknamed 'River Stink' locally, yet there were prominent men who defended the filthy state of the town, and one Councillor Baxendale called smoke a good thing, deservedly being satirised for his ignorance by a local poet. Dickens himself satirises this attitude of northern mill-masters in *Hard Times* when the notorious manufacturer, Josiah Bounderby, says to a southerner newly up from London: 'First of all, you see our smoke. That's meat and drink to us. It's the healthiest thing in the world in all respects, and particularly for the lungs. If you are one of those who want to consume it, I differ from you. We are not going to wear the bottoms of our boilers out any faster than we wear 'em out now, for all the humbugging sentiment in Great Britain and Ireland'.

Bounderby in many ways typifies the Bradford industrialist of this period and Dickens drew on his recollections and experiences of northern visits to Bradford and the surrounding area for many of his character studies in *Hard Times* and elsewhere. Dickens was first in Bradford in 1854 and knew the appalling state many of the northern and midland industrial towns had fallen into. Baxendale may not have contributed to the character of Bounderby, but Bounderby is certainly the epitome of Baxendale and his type who, unfortunately for Bradford, held a great deal of power in governing the town's affairs early on in the nineteenth century.

Strikes and riots were common in Bradford between 1821 and 1847 when employment fluctuated greatly and little was done to improve bad housing. The few watchmen and constables in the town – there were six in 1840 for a population of over 65,000 – were hopelessly inadequate and the military were frequently called in. In 1825 the textile workers in the town went on strike for twenty-two weeks and nearly 20,000 operatives were thrown out of work in the area. Nearly £16,000 was spent in relieving over 6,000 people affected by the strike, a considerable sum of money in 1825. The main reason for the strike finally ending was the absconding of the union leader, John Tester, with the strike funds! Most of the strikers were hand-craftsmen and their outstanding complaint was not against bad housing or bad working conditions, but against the introduction of steam-powered machinery in the mills.

In 1822 a Bradford manufacturer, James Warbrick, bought a power-loom and had it sent secretly to a mill at Shipley. News soon leaked out of its arrival, however, and a great number of handloom weavers gathered together outside the mill and threatened to burn it down unless the loom was removed. The loom was hastily put back into a cart and guarded by constables for its removal. However, the mob rushed the cart and the constables fled, leaving the loom to be destroyed by the weavers, who dragged its broken warp in triumph through Baildon.

A more serious riot took place on 1 May 1826 in Bradford itself, after a meeting of unemployed workmen took place on Fairweather Green. About 250 of them marched on Horsfall's Mill near the Parish Church intending to break up some power-looms which had been installed in the mill. They were prevented from entering the mill, however, and merely stoned the windows at first. They then went to Bradford Moor, about a mile on the Leeds Road, where they were joined by 200 more, and with these reinforcements they returned to the mill and made a second attack. However the Riot Act was read and the mob later dispersed. Two days later a larger meeting was held on Fairweather Green and again the crowd went to Horsfall's Mill where they began throwing stones. They completely demolished three of the windows but were unable to force an entry. The Riot Act was again read but the mob continued throwing stones. Shots were fired and two persons were killed with several wounded. Two of the rioters were sent to York Castle.

Because there were no regular barracks in Bradford, as there were in Leeds, there was more inclination for the disaffected workers in Bradford to riot. There were serious anti-Poor Law riots in 1837 when there was hand-to-hand fighting between the workers and the 15th Hussars. There were Chartist riots in 1839 after the Chartists had openly drilled on Fairweather Green, and a group of plug-drawers from Bradford moved on to Leeds in 1842 after going on the rampage in Bradford. There were Orange (Anti-Catholic) riots in 1844 and further Chartist riots in 1848 when many people were wounded in a clash with the militia.

But Bradford life in the early part of the nineteenth century was not entirely sordid. More civilizing institutions, in education, social work, the arts and sciences, were founded by the more responsible elements of the township's population.

Richard Oastler, a Leeds man, campaigned for many years against the terrible conditions and long hours which children had to suffer during their work in the textile mills. In 1830, John Wood, of Horton Hall, was senior partner in a textile firm and, like the Salt family, was one of the few Bradford manufacturers who were genuinely concerned for the welfare of their workers. He was especially concerned about the long hours children were compelled to work in the growing number of Bradford mills run by men less caring than himself. As early as 1825 Wood maintained that ten hours was as long as any mill-master ought to expect an operative to work. In 1830 he invited Richard Oastler to see for himself the conditions in Bradford mills and after a long interview with Oastler, Wood said, 'I cannot allow you to leave me without a pledge that you will use all your influence in endeavouring to remove from our factory system the cruelties which are now regularly practised.'

Oastler gave his pledge and spent a lifetime trying to bring about reform and stop the exploitation of young children. The Poor Law, with its degrading abuses, also became a target for his relentless criticism. On 30 September 1830, Edward Baines, a journalist and himself a leading protagonist of social reform in Yorkshire, printed Oastler's famous letter in *The Leeds Mercury*, a letter which drew attention to the slavery of young children in the mills:

> ... a state of slavery more horrid than ... that hellish system, colonial slavery. The
> very streets are every morning wet by the tears of innocent victims at the accursed
> shrine of avarice who are compelled not by the cast-whip of the negro slave-driver,
> but by the equally appalling thong or strap of the overlooker to hasten, half-dressed

but not half-fed, to those magazines of British infantile slavery, the worsted mills
... Thousands of little children, both male and female, but principally female,
from seven to fourteen years of age, are daily compelled to labour from six in the
morning to seven in the evening ... with only thirty minutes allowed for eating and
recreation.

The letter raised a storm of reaction against Oastler and several manufacturers defended the long working hours of children, claiming that work kept them off the streets and encouraged learning skills. But it also aroused the conscience of other more charitable men and eventually led to a movement which brought about the passing of the Ten Hours Act in 1847. Richard Oastler is still commemorated in Bradford by his statue, depicting him succouring two mill-children.

William Edward Forster was another Bradford reformer who gained world-wide fame in education. He arrived in Bradford in 1841, a young Quaker from Dorset, and was aghast at the poor social conditions he found and the lack of educational facilities. He sympathised strongly with the Chartist Movement and eventually became Member of Parliament for Bradford in 1865. Being married to the daughter of the famous headmaster, Dr Arnold of Rugby, it is not surprising that his energies should be directed at educational reform. He was also a great friend of Thomas Carlyle, who came to Bradford on occasions as his guest. Forster's great contribution to the development of English society was his successful introduction of the Elementary Education Bill into Parliament which was passed as the Education Act of 1871. Through the terms of this Bill the first elementary state schools, the Board Schools, were established by a levy on local rates. The nation's children were able to receive for the first time some sort of rudimentary education which had been denied the children of the working classes for so long. Although it was years before Board Schools were built in many parts of the country, Forster's Act gave local authorities the first opportunity to set up elementary state schools if they wished.

Despite having a population of over 40,000 in 1831, there was little opportunity for the mass of Bradford people to pursue even very elementary education. Indeed, there was downright hostility on the part of many of its educated citizens towards any movement which forwarded education of the workers. In many other respects, too, Bradford had fallen well behind many northern towns in the provision and development of civic amenities. It was left to more enlightened minds later on in the century to try and make good the deficiencies so painfully obvious in the first half of the nineteenth century.

In 1830 Bradford still had no newspaper, although *The Leeds Mercury* had been founded as early as 1718. Gas lighting had only recently reached some of its streets and steam power was only just being adopted in its mills. There was no rail communication and Bradford travellers still had to use the stagecoach. There was, above all, opposition to attempts at social development. Men like Oastler, and civic committees such as the Commissioners sat on, met constant hostility, and often from persons in high authority.

The Vicar of Bradford, the Revd Henry Heap, for example, opposed the formation of a Mechanics' Institute because he thought it would give the workers ideas above their station. He predicted it would become 'a seminary of disaffection, and a nursery of political demagogues and anarchists'. He was not alone in his views; indeed, opposition to public education continued well into the 1870s when a special mass-meeting was convened in St George's Hall to protest about the provision of schools in Bradford which educated the poor and which had to be paid for from the rates.

Nevertheless, the few people in Bradford with the real interests of the town at heart pushed forward despite the reaction they encountered. The Mechanics' Institute was founded on 14 February 1832 and opened in a rented room in Piccadilly, moving from there to a variety of places until it occupied its own buildings in 1840. It went from strength to strength as the century progressed, being patronised by men like Benjamin Seebohm, head of a German immigrant family which did much to raise the cultural tone of Bradford in the nineteenth century. The Mechanics' Institute was not lacking in support either from the men it set out to educate and in the first year 352 artisans enrolled for classes in basic education. Titus Salt was also a liberal patron of the Institute and did much to clear it from the debt which had arisen when it built its own premises in 1840. So rapid was the Mechanics' Institute's growth after 1850 that new premises had to be built and a more enlightened group of city elders soon found the necessary money to start the building. Its foundation stone was laid in 1870 and the building was completed in the October of the following year and opened by W.E. Forster himself as Minister of Education. Many famous lecturers visited the Bradford Mechanics' Institute to read papers there, including H.M. Stanley, the American journalist who contacted Livingstone in Africa, W.M. Thackeray, the novelist and literary critic, and John Ruskin, the art critic.

The first Bradford newspaper, *The Bradford Courier and West Riding Advertiser*, appeared in 1825. It was primarily a political newspaper floated by a group of

A fair outside the long-gone Christ Church at the top of Darley Street. (Bradford Libraries)

Tory businessmen and it lasted about three years. It cost a considerable sum
of money, at 7d a copy, and families often clubbed together to buy their daily
paper. The rival political party of the time, the Whigs, set up their newspaper
nine days after the Tories. It was called *The Bradford and Wakefield Chronicle*
and it had a shorter lifespan even than its rival, lasting just nine months and
one week! No more Bradford newspapers were founded until 1834, when
The Bradford Observer (later *The Yorkshire Observer*) was first issued, and in
the interim the two Leeds papers, *The Mercury* and *The Intelligencer*, supplied
Bradford with news. William Byles came to Bradford from the Athenaeum to
edit the newspaper and it was through his guidance it became a morning daily
in 1868. The *Bradford Daily Telegraph* came into being as an evening daily on
16 July 1868, when it was founded by Thomas Shields and has been published
continuously since and is now Bradford and district's premier paper (combining
with the *Bradford Argus* to become the *Telegraph & Argus*).

The 1820s saw the creation of many typical Bradford institutions. The first
market hall was opened in Kirkgate in 1824 and a dispensary, the forerunner of
Bradford Infirmary, was founded the same year in a house near Church Bank.
The following year the first Roman Catholic Church, St Mary's on the Mount,
was opened along with Eastbrook Methodist Chapel.

Schools

Education of the masses was very much frowned upon in Bradford during the
first three decades of the last century. We have seen what opposition there was
to the founding of a Mechanics' Institute and similarly there was opposition to
start any educational establishments at all for primary education.

Apart from the grammar school and the Airedale College, which began life
about the 1750s as 'Mr Scott's Academy', there was no cheap education in

The General Infirmary, erected
1843. (Bradford Libraries)

Bradford Grammar School,
1830. (Bradford Libraries)

Bradford for youngsters until the Sunday schools became well established. Many middle-class Bradfordians thought it was dangerous educating the operatives and, indeed, in the report of the Kirkgate Wesleyan Sunday school for 1817, there is a kind of apology for the instruction going on there, an apology to those who believed 'education would make the lower orders of society less disposed to submit to the constituted authorities and to act in a subordinate capacity'. Most of the youngsters attending the Sunday schools were illiterate mill-children who snatched what little education they could on their only day off work. After working often twelve hours a day and being in the mills from 6.00 a.m. to 7.00 or 8.00 p.m., one is amazed at the numbers of children, voluntarily or not, attending Bradford Sunday schools.

In 1822, for example, the Parish Church Sunday School annual account stated that the total number of scholars for the year was 419, an increase of more than a hundred on the previous year. The salary James Speight, the schoolmaster, was paid for coping with this number of youngsters was £6 9s 5d. It seemed that several Sunday schools had professional teachers then, though most of the elementary instruction was done by voluntary staff, sometimes in the most primitive conditions. Letters of the alphabet were taught by the finger being drawn across a tray of sand, or words were formed by sliding wooden letters along a couple of bars.

There were, however, a number of other societies endeavouring to promote education among the poor. Foremost among these educationists were the Quakers, who established the Quakers' School in 1816 and later built a larger school in Chapel Street, Leeds Road, in 1831. Two hundred boys, 140 girls and 130 infants were on the rolls when the new Quakers' School was opened – not very many out of the town's total population of nearly 44,000 at that time.

The Bradford historian and educationist, Dr Scoresby, started a Parochial School Fund in 1839 and with the money collected by that fund church schools were subsequently opened at the Model School, Manchester Road, the New Leeds School, the Daisy Hill School, the Church School at Eccleshill and a school at Stott Hill. Five other church schools were eventually opened in Bradford between 1839 and 1846 which educated over 3,000 Bradford children a year.

Parliament

1832 was an important year in the history of Bradford for it was in this year that Bradford returned its first Members of Parliament. Under the Reform Act of 1832 Bradford was made a Parliamentary Borough and was allowed to nominate two Members. Nine hundred and sixty seven people were allowed to vote and two social reformers were elected as Bradford's first MPs, Ellis Cunliffe Lister, a Whig, and John Hardy, also a Whig, who defeated the only other candidate, a Tory called George Banks of Leeds, who supported the Ten Hours' Bill.

German Influence

The 1830s also saw the influx of a sizeable German merchant class into Bradford. In 1834 a German trader called Jacob Behrens came to Leeds to establish an export business in cloth to the Continent. Four years later he moved to Bradford and established a warehouse in Thornton Road and began what was to be an era of cultural as well as commercial development in Bradford which

Election time at the White Lion Inn, Kirkgate. (Bradford Libraries)

stemmed from its German community. Behrens died in 1889, having made a fortune. German immigration into the West Riding towns had started in the late 1820s and grew considerably over the next few decades, especially in Bradford. In 1827 there were no foreign worsted merchants in either Leeds or Bradford, though trade was very strong with the Continent. By 1837 there were seven foreign merchants in Leeds and eight in Bradford; ten years later there were thirty-four in Bradford and by the 1860s there were at least sixty-five German firms trading in Bradford, part of which became known as Little Germany. In 1864 Bradford had a German-born Mayor, Charles Semon, and Jacob Moser, who had come from Schleswig Holstein, was another (in 1910).

This influx of highly intelligent German families played an important role in the cultural development of the city, as well as its financial one. They brought with them long traditions of European music, art and literature and raised considerably the cultural status of the embryo city. The composer Frederick Delius came from this German immigrant stock and was born in Bradford in 1862, receiving his early education at the grammar school in Bradford before leaving an unwilling apprenticeship to the wool trade and making his way in

The (old) Theatre Royal in Duke Street, c. 1845. There is a plaque commemorating the theatre at the site today. (Bradford Libraries)

the world as a composer. In the realms of Bradford music Sir Jacob Behrens also played an important part by helping to inaugurate the subscription concerts and inviting Charles Hallé from Manchester to play at them.

Another great Bradford industrialist to make his name in the 1830s was Titus Salt, who made his fortune by using alpaca wool with cotton warps. Today Sir Titus Salt is more renowned for the model-village he created for his workers at Saltaire in the 1850s and '60s, well clear of the filth and dirt to be found in the Bradford of that time. But in the 1830s, he revolutionized the worsted trade by developing the use of alpaca weft and cotton warps.

The alpaca wool was brought to Titus Salt's mills in Bradford and turned into some of the finest cloth sent out of the city. It also revolutionized the production of worsted cloth and Salt's fortune was made.

From Town to Borough

The 1840s and '50s were stirring times in Bradford's development. These were the decades when much of the work was put in to make Bradford the great city it became by the end of the century. Civic pride at last began to make itself felt among the merchants whose businesses were in Bradford, and in 1842 moves were started to make Bradford a borough with its own mayor and council. Those wanting the establishment of a corporation met in the Mechanics' Institute and drafted a petition for Parliament which was signed by 56 merchants, 93 woolstaplers, 220 worsted manufacturers, 60 innkeepers, 16 Nonconformist ministers, 13 solicitors, 13 doctors, 13 dyers, 2 bankers, 2,100 shopkeepers and 8,187 workpeople. The petition was also supported by most of the old board of Lighting and Watching Commissioners and twelve out of the thirteen surveyors.

Yet, as in the neighbouring city of Leeds, there was a strong reactionary group led by the Anglican Church who bitterly opposed municipal reform, doubtless because much power would be taken out of their hands. The vicar and 8 parsons opposed it, together with 11 West Riding Magistrates, 21 solicitors, 3 bankers, 2 physicians, 18 surgeons, the Low Moor and Bowling Iron Companies and various other groups including 98 innkeepers, 1,003 shopkeepers and 10,535 workpeople.

chapter six

From Borough to City: 1847-1898

Taking the general condition of Bradford, I am obliged to pronounce it to be the most filthy town I have visited and I see no symptoms of any improvement in the more recent arrangements for the abodes of the working classes.

(1845. 'Report on the Sanitary Condition of Bradford' by James Smith.)

The mess that Bradford had got itself into is not surprising for no single body was responsible for dealing with the problems in an organised way. There was a rather ramshackle and inefficient mixture of several separate bodies comprising the Lord of the Manor, the Vestry, the Magistracy, the Lighting and Watching Commission, the Highway Surveyors, Poor Law Guardians and the Improvement Commission. Their powers were limited, most met in secret (if at all), levied separate rates and were not on good terms with each other.

The townships of Bowling, Manningham, Horton and Bradford were such close neighbours that whatever one did affected the others and it was obvious that they ought to combine forces for the common good. So a public meeting of ratepayers was called at which it was decided to make application to the Privy Council for a Charter of Incorporation. Incorporation meant that a town had the right to elect a council, to levy rates and to publish accounts. The decision was opposed by some of the Commissioners and Surveyors, who wished to retain their authority, so a government inquiry was held to consider the whole question. When a vote was taken, the objectors won, but those in favour continued to campaign and the decision later went in their favour. In April 1847, Queen Victoria signed the Charter giving Bradford permission to elect a mayor, fourteen aldermen, and forty-two councillors. Henceforth, the inhabitants of the new borough were to be 'for ever one body politic and corporate in deed, fact and name'.

Since a councillor had to have £1,000-worth of property or to be rated at £30 a year, and only 5,457 of Bradford's population of 66,718 had sufficient qualifications to vote for a new council, power remained amongst a relatively small clique of powerful men.

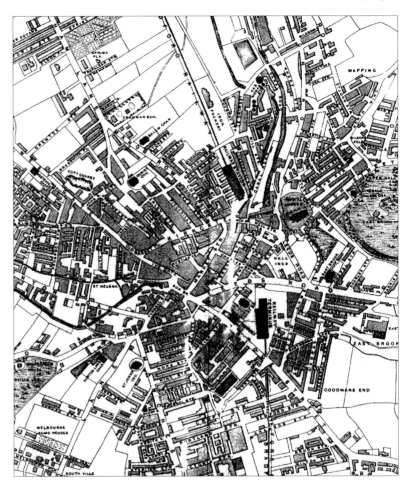

Extract from J. Rapkin's map of Bradford, c. 1854. The built-up area was creeping outwards. (Bradford Libraries)

A general view of Bradford from the north, c. 1866. Chimneys are beginning to dominate. (John James, *Continuation and Additions to the History of Bradford*, 1866. Courtesy Bradford Libraries)

The first Mayor was Robert Milligan, a partner in the firm of Milligan, Forbes & Company (whose warehouse is now used by the *Telegraph & Argus* newspaper) and the new council established itself in the former Commissioner's House in Swaine Street, which it shared with the Watch and the town's fire engine.

On the new Bradford Coat of Arms, the three horns stood for the three calls John Northrop gave to welcome the Lord of the Manor; the sprouting tree above the boar's head represented Cliffe Wood; the well the drinking place there; and the boar, always without a tongue, was based on the legendary story of the boar's killing. The motto was *Labor Omnia Vincit*, Work Conquers All.

The new borough administration appeared to have had able and conscientious staff, but the resources were poor and the problems huge.

In 1843, the *Bradford Observer* noted that Bradford was 'infested with thieves and vagabonds, the doors of its inhabitants besieged with beggars, whilst riot, drunkenness and street-fighting is carried on with impunity'. Clearly the establishment of a police force was an early priority for the new council, so a chief constable, two superintendents, two inspectors, six sergeants and sixty-one police constables were appointed.

The ever-increasing population, exacerbated by the influx of Irish due to the potato famine of 1845-46, was the most pressing problem that faced the new council. Overcrowding was commonplace. The Woolcombers' Report of 1845 recorded instances of the use of buildings to house farm animals, the lack of drainage, and the seepage of household refuge and excrement into cellar dwellings. It was not uncommon for sick people, and even the dead, to be lying in the same room in which wool-combing was being carried on. In his first report to the Borough Council, the Surveyor wrote that, 'Notwithstanding the effort of your Committee, great numbers of dwellings for the labouring classes are still built back-to-back in courts, with a semi-circular dwelling beneath, a circumstance very much to be regretted as it must be evident that proper and

left Establishing a police force was one of the first things the new Bradford Corporation did. This policeman was photographed in around 1890. (Bradford Libraries)

below Back-to-back housing, midden privies and cellars, location unknown. (Bradford Heritage Recording Unit. Courtesy Bradford Libraries)

Above left: Back-to-back housing, Jonas Gate, in the 1930s. (Bradford Libraries)

Above right: Sir Titus Salt. This statue was re-erected in Lister Park in 1896, having previously stood outside the Town Hall.

effective provision of a sanitary character cannot be maintained under these conditions'. Generally there were no drains and 'There are upwards of 500 streets within the Borough, one third of which are almost impassable'. He called for more stringent control of 'building speculators'.

Building bye-laws were produced in 1853 and revised in 1860, but the officials were too few and they got little support from their elected employers. Many of these employers, of course, lived in the many elegant houses which were being built to advertise the civic pride of Bradford's public men. The Building and Improvement Committee first banned the back-to-backs in 1854, but this was lifted in 1865 in the face of fierce opposition. However, strict new regulations were introduced and enlightened mill-owners such as Titus Salt and Henry Ripley made improvements in areas where they had influence. A bye-law of 1875 prohibited the occupation of a new house until its drainage was complete and it had been approved by the medical Officer of Health. Cellar dwellings became a thing of the past and streets were widened. In 1877 the corporation began a programme of slum clearance with the demolition of eighty houses in Silsbridge Lane.

The more affluent, of course, lived in their better-off enclaves in Little Horton, Manningham and Heaton, as well as in the stylish Victorian squares such as Apsley Crescent and Hanover Square. Gary Firth, in his *History of Bradford*, quotes a remark by a 1861 census enumerator that in the St Paul's Road area of Manningham 'there are many houses of superior class occupied by the principal families in the district'. By the 1880s there was also a drift out to the suburbs, though in fact the pressure on housing was falling as the birth rate fell. In 1890, the Housing and Working Classes Act was passed which empowered councils to clear slum areas and ushered in the era of council housing.

A great deal of street clearance and re-building was carried out. In the central area, Sunbridge Road and Bank Street were established, and the Kirkgate

above left An age of elegance. Mrs Cunliffe, village doctor's wife, and Mr Charles Richardson, coachman, at Elm House, Clayton, 1900. (Bradford Libraries)

above right Nursemaid and pram, c. 1890. (Bradford Libraries)

left Victorian terraced housing, Bradford Moor.

covered market was built. So also was the warehouse precinct known as 'Little Germany' with its architectural mix of Classical and Gothic styles. The inner suburbs were by now completely joined to the town centre and a number of elegant Victorian squares and quiet spacious streets were constructed. The largest area of in-filling of the spaces between the roads radiating out from the centre was given over to the thousands of mass-built working 'bye-law' back-to-backs and terrace houses. Between 1860 and 1873, back-to-backs were permitted subject to minimum space and other requirements. After 1873 they were prohibited and the terrace became the typical form of low-priced housing. Working-class houses of this period usually had backyards, possibly their own privy and ashpit, with a rear access road. Many of these houses survive today.

Although incorporation allowed the Corporation to establish a police force, it still had no authority to deal with public health or improvement and there was no shortage of vested interests that opposed giving it wider powers. Malnutrition, over-crowding and a heavily polluted atmospheric and water environment contributed to high death rates; infants accounted for about half the total deaths per year. There were epidemics of Asian Cholera in 1833 and 1848-49, yet the deaths resulting from these were less than the number of children who died from diseases such as diarrhoea and scarlatina. Tuberculosis was another major killer. The dead were disposed of in the ancient cemeteries which lay in the inner built-up area until the opening of the private cemetery at Undercliffe in 1852.

The outbreak of cholera in 1849, which caused 420 deaths, weakened the resistance of vested interests and saw an increase in the powers given to the council to improve public health. Providing a reliable supply of pure water was critical for this and the privately owned waterworks company who had a reservoir in Westgate was clearly failing to provide this. The Corporation bought the company in 1854 and assumed responsibility to supply water. But in 1858 supplies ran out and the townspeople were reduced to using wells or buying from barrels. More local reservoirs were constructed but local water resources were insufficient for Bradford's needs and it was only in the early twentieth century, when reservoirs were built in Nidderdale, that the city got an adequate water supply.

In 1864 an attempt was made to put in sewers, but even that was merely to pipe the untreated sewage further downstream. Main sewers were constructed along the White Abbey, Thornton and Horton Roads and between Leeds Road and Wapping. The waters which drained from the streams of Bradford Dale emptied into the canal basin. These streams carried the effluent of dyehouses, the grease, dung and soapy wastes from scouring houses, and the washings from the fouled streets, as well as household waste. The escape of gas from this source was said to be so considerable that it would discolour the silver in the houses and workshops nearby.

The old canal basin was closed and by 1870 over thirty miles of new sewers had been built. A water purification plant was built in Manningham in 1872, and a larger sewage treatment works in 1889. The Bradford Beck continued to

An unflattering view of Bradford. Note the Canal Basin and the Bradford Beck above it. (*Illustrated London News*, 24 June 1882. Courtesy Bradford Libraries)

be used as a sewer, but when the owner of Esholt Hall complained of the beck fouling the River Aire, the council purchased the Esholt estate and constructed a large sewage treatment works there!

Other public health developments by the council were the opening of a public cemetery at Scholemoor in 1877 to augment the private cemetery at Undercliffe run by the Bradford Cemetery Company, and the collection and controlled tipping of dry refuse in 1887.

Smoke pollution was another serious problem, but this the Corporation failed to tackle, largely because of the strength of vested interests. The failure to build chimneys to a minimum height of 30 yards was the most frequent breech of the byelaws. The Corporation had more success in creating public parks. Peel Park had been opened as a public space in 1852 and was bought by the Corporation in 1863. Lister Park (a former deer park) was opened in 1870, followed by

Another view of smoking chimneys. George Hodgson's Beehive Mills on Longside Lane. Mr Hodgson was a power-loom maker and iron founder. (G. Measom, *Official Guide to the G. N. Railway*. Courtesy Bradford Libraries)

Bowling Moor Cemetery. Bradford Corporation was responsible for establishing a number of cemeteries.

Horton Park (1878), Bowling Park (1880), Heaton Woods (1882), Bradford Moor Park (1884) and, with the extension of Bradford's boundaries, Harold Park (Low Moor) (1881) and Wibsey Park (1885). A number of recreation grounds were also established. Away from the smoke-laden air of Bradford, these areas of open land were popular recreational spaces.

We have seen how the Corporation was obliged to buy up the private water company and initiate work on drainage, sewerage and rubbish collection. In 1871 the town's private gas supply was purchased by the Corporation and in 1889 Bradford became the first place in the country to provide a municipal electricity supply.

By these measures, Bradford was becoming a healthier place to live and cholera, typhus, typhoid and smallpox had virtually disappeared by the end of the century. The Bradford Infirmary was built in Westgate in 1843.

In the second half of the nineteenth century, working conditions improved, the hours of work reduced, and wages had increased. Generally, the population were better-off. For the poor, however, there was always the Poor Law. The unsatisfactory nature of the old Poor Law legislation had provided fuel for the anti-Poor Law riots in the town in 1837. In 1848 the Poor Law Commissioners had insisted upon the creation of a Bradford Borough Union and another for the outlying areas, the North Bierley Union. A deep recession in the worsted trade, a widespread typhus epidemic and a larger than usual influx of Irish vagrants necessitated the building of a new workhouse. This was opened in 1851 on the site of the present St Luke's Hospital. The building was later extended to accommodate 900 inmates. There was a workhouse medical centre, pauper school and lunatic asylum. By the 1880s there were 650 inmates, mostly orphans, the aged and the insane.

Education was another area where great changes were being made and the quality of life was being improved. Forster's 1870 Education Act replaced the unsatisfactory mix of private and philanthropic factory schools, charity schools,

below left The Bradford Eye and Ear Hospital, Hallfield Road, established 1857. (Annual Report, 1905. Courtesy Bradford Libraries)

below right Bradford from Undercliffe. A sketch of Victorian ladies and gentlemen parading in 1865. (*Bradford Times*, 24 June 1865. Courtesy Bradford Libraries)

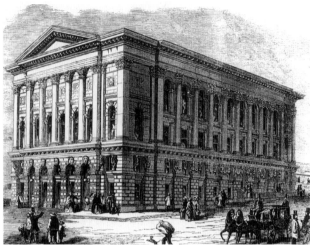

above left The statue of W.E. Forster in Forster Square.

above right St George's Hall, opened 1853. (*Illustrated London News*, 3 September 1853)

right Inside the Wool Exchange, 1986, when it was used for the Flea Market. It was built in 1867 for the buying and selling of wool. (Bradford Heritage Recording Unit)

and Sunday schools with compulsory schooling for all children up to the age of fourteen. School Boards were established which were empowered to raise money from the rates and fill gaps in the education provided by voluntary schemes. By 1885, 24,000 children were receiving elementary education through the Board Schools. Under the leadership of Margaret McMillan, free school meals and milk, the use of school baths and the introduction of school medical inspections were introduced in the 1890s.

The new civic authorities were conscious of the need to establish their identity and, following the examples of Leeds, Manchester and Liverpool, a number of new public buildings were constructed. The public subscribed to a fund to build St George's Hall, which was opened in 1853. Designed to serve as a cultural centre, it was soon being used to hold monthly council meetings, the Corporation's Station House now being too small. In 1865, the Wool Exchange was completed and opened by the Prime Minister, Lord Palmerston. Both buildings were designed by the Bradford architects, Lockwood & Mawson. The former 'frontier town' was becoming civilised!

In 1869, it was decided to build a town hall and an 'Invitation for Competitive Design' was advertised. The 'Schedule of Particulars' is interesting since it lists the space required by the growing army of municipal officers and services. These included:

Town Hall Curator
Fire Brigade and fire engine
Police Department and twenty-six cells for prisoners

Weights and Measures Department

Markets Superintendent

Inspector of Hackney Carriages and Lamps

Inspector of Nuisances

Scavenging Department

Smoke and Workshop Inspector

Borough Surveyor

Borough Accountant

Borough Collector

Waterworks Engineer

Drawing Office (for Borough Surveyor)

Town Clerk

Committee Rooms

Mayor's Apartments

Magistrates Officers

Borough Court

Overseers and Guardians

Grand Jury

Recorder

Council Chamber

Architect's drawing of the new Town Hall. (*Illustrated London News*, 20 September 1873. Courtesy Bradford Libraries)

Living and sleeping quarters were required by the Curator and the Fire Brigade Superintendent. (Details from *Bradford City Hall: A History and Guide* by Michael Leslie, 1997)

The competition was won by the local firm of Lockwood & Mawson. The winning design was in the Gothic style, then much in vogue. The frontage was 275 feet long with three gables, one at the centre and one at each end. The tower is massive, rising to 217 feet, and based on the campanile of the Palazzo Vecchio in Florence. The foundation stone was laid in August 1870 and the builders were John Ives & Son of Shipley. The stone is local Gaisby rock from the Cliffe Wood quarries. The building was opened with great ceremony on 9 September 1873 and cost close on £100,000. In a heated argument over the cost of a clock, chimes and carillon, Mayor Matthew Thompson closed the debate by claiming that, 'They did not live in Bradford merely for the purpose of making money, but also to improve the place, to improve themselves, and to elevate the condition of the people'. Even despite this appeal to higher ideals, the Mayor had to use his casting vote.

By 1884, the number of Corporation departments had risen to twenty-four and land was purchased at the rear of the Town Hall to build an extension, though building work did not start until 1905, by which time Bradford had become a city.

Detail from the Town Hall, now City Hall.

Wrote Barbara Castle in her autobiography, *Fighting All The Way* (1993):

> Bradford was an impressive city ... and I soon responded to the grandeur of the
> solid stone buildings in the city centre, dominated by the Town Hall. This imposing
> stone edifice had been erected in 1873 when Joseph Chamberlain was raising
> the banner of municipal enterprise in Birmingham. In those pre-Thatcherite days
> people of all parties in our big towns had a sense of civic pride and nowhere more
> than in Bradford, where the rough, blunt Yorkshire businessman made it clear they
> were not going to be pushed around by Whitehall.

Bradford was fortunate to have a succession of forceful mayors and public-spirited industrialists. Although great wealth was being generated by the mill owners, much of this wealth found its way back into the community in the form of public buildings and the foundation of charitable and educational institutions. Notable figures include:

• Samuel Cunliffe Lister, Lord Masham, whose innovations and inventions in textiles made him a millionaire. He gave £50,000 to the cost of building the Cartwright Memorial Hall and donated the 52 acres of the grounds of his house to the Corporation in 1870.
• Sir Titus Salt (Mayor 1848-49). Though best known for his mills at Saltaire, Salt's earlier mills were in Bradford and he was Bradford's MP from 1859 to 1861. Apart from his work to improve the lot of his workers, there is barely an institution in Bradford which does not have Salt as a benefactor.
• Samuel Smith (Mayor 1851-54), founder of the extensive dyeworks at Field Head in Thornton Road, was instrumental in getting Bradford linked directly to Wakefield by rail. His interest in music saw him laying the foundation stone for St George's Hall and president of the Bradford Festival Chorus Society.
• Henry Brown (Mayor 1856-59), a prosperous draper and clothier (he was later to become the Brown of Brown, Muff & Co.), created the Bradford Tradesmen's Benevolent Institution, gave £6,000 towards the endowment of scholarships at Bradford Grammar School and was one of the promoters of the Undercliffe Cemetery Company.
• Isaac Wright (Mayor 1859-62) was a wool stapler, Treasurer of the Bradford Exchange Buildings and Newsrooms, a member of the management of the Infirmary and chairman of the Waterworks Committee.
• Charles Semon (Mayor 1864-66) was prominent in the wool trade. He was generous to local charities, helped to found the Eye and Ear Hospital, was governor of the Bradford Infirmary, and financed and endowed the Semon Convalescent Home at Ilkley, whose freehold he gave to Bradford Corporation.
• John V. Godwin (Mayor 1865-66) was notable for his skill in acquiring property so that much-needed street improvement could take place.
• James Law (Mayor 1867-68) made his mark in establishing the cattle market, wholesale vegetable market, abattoir and fairground in Leeds Road. The Kirkgate Market and the Mechanics' Institute also owe much to his efforts.

• Briggs Priestley (Mayor 1877-78) was a leading worsted manufacturer and was behind initial moves to set up a permanent art gallery in Bradford.

Other developments in municipal enterprise were the establishment of parks, libraries and museums. The borough became the first in the country to undertake the supply of electricity, had the first Smoke Inspector and the first Medical Officer of Health. Bradford was the first town in the country to use chloroform as an anaesthetic, as well as having the first civic music festival, the first Girls' Grammar School, the first technical classes, the first telephone service, the first electrically-driven tramcars and the first special school.

By a series of letters on 'Free Libraries, their Nature and Operations' addressed to Alderman J.V. Godwin by James Hanson, printed in the *Bradford Review* during November 1867, the Bradford public became familiar with the Public Library Acts, the first of which was passed in 1850. As a result of Hanson's advocacy, the Town Council appointed a sub-committee 'to inquire into, and report upon, the working of the Free Libraries Acts'. As required by the Act a public meeting was held in 1871, the resolution proposing the adoption being moved by Godwin, seconded by Mr (later Sir) Jacob Berens, and supported by Henry W. Ripley. Despite the opposition of those who opposed the raising of a library rate, the motion was passed.

Some rooms in Tyrrel Street were found, books donated and 183 applicants sought to be the librarian. The Reference Library and Reading Room were

Lister Park, Manningham, from *Brear's Guide to Bradford*, 1873. (Courtesy Bradford Libraries)

opened in June 1872, and the Lending Library the following February. The library was so successful that new premises were found in a new building being constructed in the Kirkgate Market in Darley Street.

Although intended solely for library use, it was decided to establish an Art Gallery and Museum and to share the building. Like the library, exhibits had to be found locally, although the Science Museum in South Kensington did lend some objects of art and a number of wall cases containing samples of textile fabrics. (The passing of the Museum Act in 1891 allowed a rate to be levied.) The library struggled for funds and the Corporation used the profits from the Gas Department to assist. Ironically, the library and museum was the first municipal building in the country to be lit by the Corporation's own electricity supply! Bradford was early in the supply of books to outlying areas, usually by using school buildings, and there were eight branch libraries in 1886 when there were half a million visits to the reading rooms. Purpose-built branch library buildings, though, were not established until the next century. The librarian, Butler Wood, doubled up as librarian and curator of the Art Gallery and Museum, and the end of the century found moves in hand to build a separate art gallery in Lister Park – the Cartwright Memorial Art Gallery.

By 1860, factory legislation had created more regular free time and the 1871 Bank Holidays Act saw Whitsuntide become a national holiday. With increased prosperity people started to develop leisure pursuits. With the railways offering cheap excursions to seaside resorts, Morecambe, Scarborough and other seaside resorts saw an annual influx of Bradford holidaymakers. Sporting clubs mushroomed: Bradford RFC in 1866, Bradford City FC in 1903 and West Bradford Cricket League in 1893. Walking and cycling became popular pastimes.

A number of other culturally related institutions were established towards the end of the century. In 1894 the Bradford Philosophical Society was 'established for the purpose of promoting the pursuit of Science, Literature and Art' by lectures, classes, libraries, exhibitions and a museum. Under the influence of the German immigrants, music and the arts flourished, and Bradford was notable for its subscription concerts, permanent symphony orchestra, two theatres, choral societies, amateur dramatics, art clubs and art gallery. A magnificent new building was opened for the Mechnics' Institute. On a popular front, music halls appeared, often, it has to be said, at the expense of the churches and chapels!

Textile mills are still a notable feature of Bradford's landscape, and they were more so in the late Victorian age. They, above all, give testimony to Bradford's Victorian heritage. Manningham Mill still dominates the Bradford skyline. It was built in 1873, replacing an earlier building destroyed by fire. The 250-foot-high Italianate chimney is a present-day icon. Daniel Illingworth's Whetley Mills is a notable building on the Thornton Road, though Henry Ripley's mill just off the Manchester Road has long since gone. It was built on old mine workings and in 1882 the 255-foot chimney crashed with the loss of fifty-four lives.

The Mechanics' Institute.
It was pulled down in the
1960s. (*The Graphic*,
20 September 1873.
Courtesy Bradford Libraries)

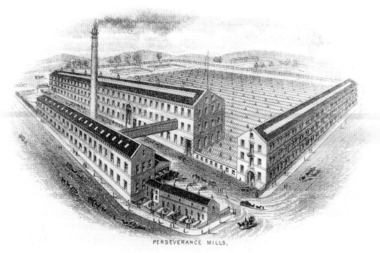

PERSEVERANCE MILLS.

Perseverance Mills, Dudley Hill
(*Industries of Yorkshire*,
c. 1888.)

Manningham Mills. (*Lord
Masham's Inventions*, 1905.)

In the last quarter of the nineteenth century the worsted trade suffered difficulties and this saw a hardening of the altruism characteristic of the earlier generation of mill-owners. This in turn sharpened the political awareness of the skilled and semi-skilled textile worker, as well as workers in other industries such as the municipal gas works, dyehouses and engineering shops. The mill dynasties were also disappearing; William Foster of Black Dyke at Queensbury, Angus Lister, Samuel Cunliffe Holden, Percy Holden Illingworth, were all heads of dynasties that turned their backs on the mills.

All this fed through into the developing political awareness of the workforce, who had been given the vote under the 1867 Reform Act. The violent five-month lock-out of 4,000 workers at Manningham Mills in 1891 became the catalyst for the working classes to form their own party. Local socialists and trade union leaders met and formed the Bradford Labour Union, later becoming the Independent Labour Party. The success of the socialist Ben Tillett at the 1892 General Election made Bradford a natural venue for the inaugural conference of the new party. Thus Bradford was the venue of the birth of the Labour Party.

Transport

Back at the start of the nineteenth century goods were transported by packhorse, horse-drawn cart or horse-drawn canal boat; coach travel and the turnpike roads were in their heyday. The earliest railway in the West Riding was the Leeds and Selby line, which opened in 1834. Travel and transport by sea was commonplace and sea-going ships could reach the port of Selby. Like the

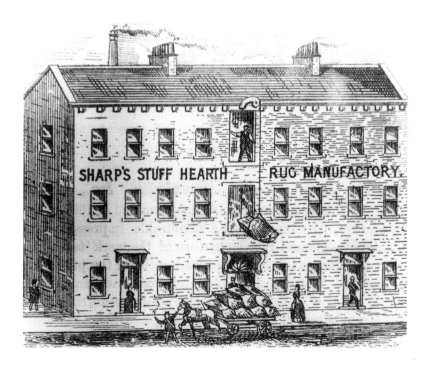

A warehouse at work. Perseverance Works, New Lane, Thornbury, c. 1893. (*The Century's Progress*, 1893. Courtesy Bradford Libraries)

businessmen of Leeds, those of Bradford thought it desirable that Bradford should be linked to Selby by rail and in 1830 efforts were made to obtain the necessary legislation. The proposal failed, largely because of the opposition of the owners of land through which the proposed railway would pass. Overtures were then made to the North Midland Company, which was building a line from Derby to Leeds, to extend their line to Bradford, but they were already fully committed. So the committee decided to form their own company and commissioned the railway engineer George Stephenson to survey a route. Stephenson concluded that a line along the Aire Valley from Leeds via Shipley would be best, especially as it would permit of further extensions to the north-west. The committee then engaged Stephenson as engineer and secured the services of George 'railway king' Hudson, MP, as chairman. The enabling Act for the Leeds & Bradford Company was passed in July 1844. The line was built along the Aire Valley route with a terminal at Wellington Street Station in Leeds, where through carriages from Bradford would connect with the Midland line to Derby, Rugby and London (Euston). The line was opened in May 1846.

The experience of going through the long Thackley Tunnel was remembered by a great-aunt of the author Horace Hird:

> One story was her experience of travelling to Kirkstall Abbey on an excursion train from Bradford which meant going through Thackley Tunnel. After the purchase of a new bonnet her coppers only bought a third-class ticket and consequently her seat was in an open-top carriage. She always remembered the terrifying whistle as the train plunged into the darkness of the tunnel, the sparks flying from the smoke-stacks of the engine, the smoke which never seemed entirely to clear away and the smarting of the eyes which it caused, the constant and heavy dripping of water from the ceiling and the noisome smell of it all. The vivid recollections of that experience remained with her all her life, likewise the remembrance of her dismay when she discovered her newly-bought bonnet was ruined. (Horace Hird, *Bradford in History*)

The other major engineering structure on this line was the thirteen-arch viaduct over what is now Apperley Lane. After a week of continuous rain, floods and high winds, it collapsed, just after the 4.50 Bradford to Leeds train had crossed over it on the afternoon of 16 November 1866. The through train service was restored in a mere six weeks! This was a period of intense competition and heavy use, and another tunnel was later needed at Thackley. In 1876 a branch to Guiseley was opened with stations at Baildon and Esholt.

The continuation of the Midland line along the Aire Valley to Keighley, Skipton and Colne opened soon after the Leeds-Bradford line had opened. An early passenger on this line was the novelist, Charlotte Brontë. In October 1849 she wrote to her friend Ellen Nussey in Birstall, suggesting meeting in Leeds unless 'it would inconvenience you to meet me there … and I will come by Bradford.' Three months later she wrote again: 'There is a train leaves Bradford at a quarter past twelve and arrives at Keighley about 34 minutes past – perhaps you had better come by that.' If Charlotte was right, and she said she had a Bradshaw timetable, a nineteen-minute rail journey from Bradford to Keighley is about the same as today, and six minutes quicker than it was in 1910 (although there were fewer stations in 1849, just Shipley and Bingley).

The story of railway development south of the city centre is a confused one. The West Riding Union Railway (absorbed by the Lancashire & Yorkshire Railway Company) constructed a line from Low Moor to Heckmondwike Junction which was opened in 1848 as part of a line to Mirfield. The same company opened a line from Low Moor to Halifax in 1850 and the important link from Low Moor to Bradford centre itself. The latter route involved the considerable engineering feats of constructing the mile-long Bowling Tunnel and the only slightly shorter Wyke Tunnel. The terminal of the L. & Y. line at Bradford (Exchange) Station was on the site of what is now the Law Courts. The stations at Bowling Junction, Low Moor and Wyke & Norwood Green have since disappeared.

In 1852 the Leeds, Bradford & Halifax Junction Railway opened an important line which linked the Manchester line to Halifax with the Great Northern line from Bradford to Leeds. From the northern end of Bowling Tunnel, it by-passed the city centre to meet the line to Leeds just short of the old Laisterdyke Station. Still prominent today is the bridge over the Wakefield Road and the level crossing on Hall Lane. The latter is now disused, but many a motorist gets a sharp bump here as it is on a steep gradient. There was a station, Bowling Bridge, just east of the Wakefield Road.

The other major railway system in the area, the Great Northern Railway, came to Bradford late. This company established a terminus at Adolphus Street (now a car park off the Wakefield Road) for its line from Leeds. This was opened in 1854. Laisterdyke became an important junction, with lines to Batley and Dewsbury and with stations at Dudley Hill and Birkenshaw & Tong opening

A preserved engine of the Lancashire & Yorkshire Railway on a visit to Haworth in 2004.

Railway crossing at Wilson
Road, Wyke. Note the trucks
on the rickety track to the left.
The rich network of works-
owned lines was a feature of
nineteenth-century Bradford.
(Bradford Libraries)

in 1854. The Adolphus Street terminus was convenient for the Corporation's
wholesale produce market, but it was a stiff climb for both man and beast from
the city centre. This was remedied twelve years later when the Great Northern
overcame some fearsome engineering problems to run their line down to the
Exchange station. The steep gradient (1:59), massive retaining walls, double
curve and seven bridges – two sharply skewed – are evidence remaining today
of this engineering hurdle.

The Great Northern was responsible for two further lines which joined up the
more isolated villages and outlying communities. A line connecting Laisterdyke
with Shipley joined up the communities of Idle, Eccleshill and Thackley in
1875. Through passenger trains beyond Shipley never materialised but there
was heavy freight and mineral traffic, especially for limestone for the Bowling
and Low Moor ironworks which came from Skipton, and the much-demanded
Idle Moor stone. The other GN branch line was originally the brainchild of
William Foster of Queensbury, who proposed a line from City Road to Thornton,
but the GN had a more ambitious scheme. In 1878 its scenic line to Halifax and
Keighley was opened, running from Exchange station with stops at Manchester
Road, Horton Park, Great Horton, Clayton, Queensbury, Thornton, and, beyond
the Bradford boundary, to Denholme, Cullingworth, Ingrow and Keighley. By
the end of the century the railways were providing a transport system which
enabled people to live further out from the centre of the city, further up the
valleys in places like Thornton, Clayton and Birkenshaw, and providing easy
travel to London and elsewhere.

The railways were augmented by a number of tram services. Bradford's
first municipally owned horse-drawn tramway system began in 1882 along
Manningham Lane and in 1898 the Corporation opened its first electric
tramway between Forster Square and Bolton Junction via Bolton Road. By
1903 the Corporation electric trams, using overhead wires, had replaced the

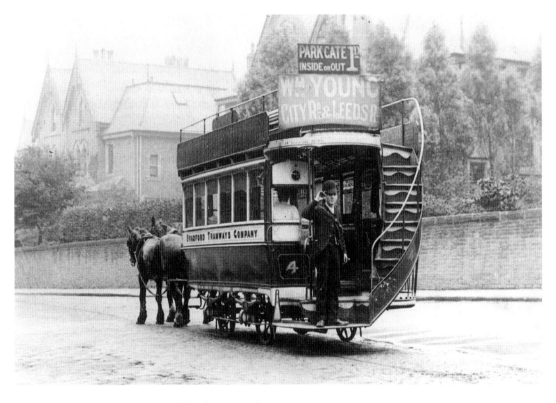

Horse tram no. 4 at Lister Park terminus. (Bradford Libraries)

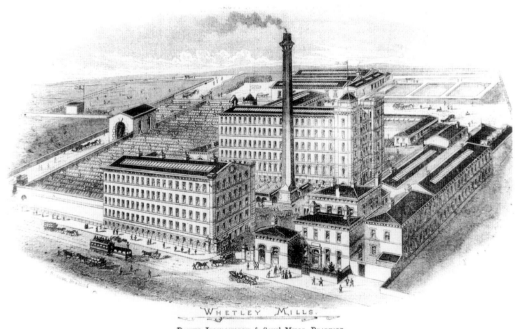

WHETLEY MILLS.

DANIEL ILLINGWORTH & SONS' MILLS, BRADFORD.

A steam tram passes in front of Daniel Illingworth & Sons' mills on Thornton Road, *c.* 1893. (*The Century's Progress.* Courtesy Bradford Libraries)

steam and horse trams previously operated by private companies. The system developed up to 1914 by which time it had reached a total of fifty-nine miles of track with services to Leeds, Drighlington, Bailiff Bridge and Crossflats. Despite differences in the track gauge, a through service operated between Leeds and Bradford. Trams were remarkable movers of crowds, whether at rush hours or from a cricket or football match. They provided low-cost passenger transport links between the villages and hamlets on the higher parts of Bradford Dale such as Heaton, Allerton, Bolton and Wyke, and the town centre. New areas of housing were developed as a consequence and possibly a stronger sense of identity with the town centre.

In 1889 Bradford was made a county borough and in 1898, to mark the fiftieth anniversary of Bradford's incorporation, the council requested Queen Victoria to grant the town city status. The request was approved. Although the elevation to city status was largely a matter of image, it does mark a stage of civic development. The success of Bradford in overcoming the problems of earlier unco-ordinated growth had encouraged many of the surrounding townships to become part of the municipality. Heaton, Allerton and Tyersal had been incorporated in 1882, and Idle, Eccleshill, North Bierley, Thornton, Tong and Wyke joined in 1897.

A tram sails along St Enoch's Road in splendid isolation. (Bradford Libraries)

chapter seven

From City to Metropolis: Twentieth-Century Bradford

The twentieth century was, above all, a century of rapid change. In 1922, the Bradford Canal closed, having played a vital part for close on 150 years in the development of Bradford as a major industrial city. The railways were at their peak, but already other forms of transport were encroaching. In 1909, the Bradford Tramways manager introduced trolleybuses, initially called the 'trackless', to use on routes with low traffic potential to feed into the tram network. The first service commenced in June 1911 along Sticker Lane between Dudley Hill and Laisterdyke, connecting two tramway corridors. Being situated in a natural bowl, most roads out of Bradford involve a steep climb: Church Bank and Whetley Hill both have a gradient steeper than 1 in 10. This fact made it unsuitable for heavy trams with poor track adhesion, but ideal for the lighter

Trolley no. 240 at Laisterdyke, 1911. (Bradford Libraries)

trolleybuses with rubber tyres. Similarly with the railways – they are good along the valley bottoms, but the bus is better elsewhere.

On a traditional note, the new century saw a new Art Gallery and Museum. In 1898, Lord Masham offered the city £40,000 for the erection of an Art Gallery and Museum to commemorate the achievement of Dr Edmund Cartwright, the inventor of the power-loom. The need for a separate art gallery had long been felt. It was a condition of the gift that the building should be erected on the site of his old house in Manningham (Lister) Park. A prolonged building trade dispute delayed matters but the new building was opened in May 1904 by the Prince and Princess of Wales. With its marble floors and grand Yorkshire stone columns, the building is an artistic masterpiece itself.

In fact the opening was part of the Bradford Exhibition held in Lister Park; a massive civic extravaganza. This featured a specially built pavilion, the Industrial Hall, in which were displayed an impressive range of textile goods and machinery made in Bradford. More popular with most of the public were the concert hall, water chute, crystal maze, gravity railway and the Somali village. Over 2.5 million people visited the exhibition during the months it was open. On the same visit, the royal couple unveiled a statue of Queen Victoria in the city centre. Again, there was a massive crowd of more than 50,000. How far off those days seem!

Cartwright Hall, Bradford's Art Gallery and Museum opened in 1904. (Bradford Libraries)

The water chute at the 1904 Bradford Exhibition in Lister Park was a popular attraction. (Bradford Libraries)

Bradford at War

The First World War marked a decisive break with the past. In the UK it marked a loss of much of the local autonomy that had been built up in the preceding decades with tighter central government control. As elsewhere, Bradford greeted the declaration of war with patriotic excitement. Crowds gathered outside Belle Vue barracks on Manningham Lane when the regular troops stationed there marched out of town; the crowds sang *Rule Britannia* and *God Save the King*. The council started classes in nursing and ambulance work, appointed a committee to check excessive food prices, raised special constables, helped the Lady Mayoress start a War Guild for making clothes to send to the troops, and arranged to receive Belgian refugees.

Recruiting began with centres established in church halls, schools and municipal premises. A Bradford Citizens' Army League was established on 20 September and the 1st Bradford Pals Battalion, officially the 16th Battalion Prince of Wales Own West Yorkshire Regiment, was recruited in a week. A second Pals Battalion (the 18th) was formed in the following February. Despite this enthusiasm there were never enough recruits and the Military Service Act introduced conscription in 1916 and Bradford's young men went to war. The dead and wounded were many. On the first day of the Battle of the Somme in 1916, the two battalions of Bradford Pals left their trenches at Sene in Picardy on the Western Front, joined the mass advance across no-man's-land, and were mown down by German machine guns. Out of 2,000 soldiers, only 223 survived. Wrote J.B. Priestley, who fought in the war (though not in the Pals):

> There are great gaps in my acquaintance now; and I find it difficult to swap reminiscences of boyhood … the men who were boys when I was a boy are dead. Indeed they never even grew to be men. They were slaughtered in youth; and the parents of them grew lonely, the girls they would have married have grown grey in spinsterhood, and the work they would have done has remained undone. (*English Journey*)

left Mobilisation. Departure from Bradford, 11 August 1914. (Tempest, *History of the 6th Battalion, West Yorkshire Regiment*, Vol. 1, p.vii. Courtesy Bradford Libraries)

below Invalided soldiers working at Westwood Farm. (Bradford Heritage Recording Unit. Courtesy Bradford Libraries)

Due in part to the slaughter of so many of its men, Bradford has had a strong peace movement. Priestley himself was a founder member of the Campaign for Nuclear Disarmament and in 1929, Norman Angell, who won an international reputation with his book *The Great Illusion* (in which he argued that war damages the victors economically) was elected MP for Bradford. The Department of Peace Studies at the university today draws students from across the world.

Bradford's war effort was also economic and was to have a lasting effect in the change from textiles to engineering. Since the enemy countries accounted for much of Bradford's export business, there was an early fear of a downturn in the textile business, but demand for serge, khaki uniforms and blankets soon proved that fear groundless. Later, with the overseas textile-producing regions disrupted, the West Riding received substantial orders from France, Serbia and Russia. Indeed, the war demanded greater productivity and longer hours, and even with the increased use of women and unskilled labour, the industry struggled to cope with the demand. Women also found jobs, not only in the traditional spinning and weaving, but in post offices, banks, warehouses, railway ticket offices and in public transport. Thus 228 women conductors were employed by the City Tramways department.

In 1914, the Low Moor Chemical Company was renamed the Low Moor Munitions Company and became the centre of the local armaments industry. It was one of many local firms that turned to manufacturing munitions. Possibly due to lax safety controls, there were a series of explosions at Low Moor on 21 August 1916 which killed thirty-eight people and injured sixty more. The explosions lasted two days and 2,000 houses were damaged. One of the more unusual products made in land-locked Bradford during the war were flying boats. Long-established furniture makers, Christopher Pratt & Sons, made the wings and fuselage (wooden ribs covered with fabric), and the Phoenix Dynamo Manufacturing Company of Thornbury made the engines. After construction in Bradford, the planes were disassembled and transported by road to the Humber, before being reassembled.

Food and fuel controls were introduced and though there was much queuing, there was never widespread deprivation. Rationing of meat, tea and butter was introduced in 1917, and prices rose – but so did wages, and the 1915 Rent Restriction Act put a brake on rent rises.

The war ended in November 1918 to general rejoicing, but it left its mark on Bradford. It was the first time that an international conflict had had such a direct effect on every individual in the town. Superficially, the textile trade remained in the hands of its paternalistic employers whose *laissez faire* attitude was unshaken, but the experience gained by organized labour working with government and employers, the influence of government controls, and the work done by women, were to have lasting implications.

The Inter-War Years, 1919-39

After 1918, woollen and worsted exports fell and the wool textile trade went into decline. This meant problems for Bradford. Employment rose at first and returning soldiers went back to their pre-war jobs, often displacing the women who had been doing them, but the underlying economic weakness soon became apparent.

A damaging dispute between the National Association of Unions in the Textile Trade (founded in 1917) and the Wool Textile Association (the employers' body) took place in 1925. The workers' side wanted to consolidate the wage increase

and improved living conditions gained during the war, while the employers were stung by the government's return to the Gold Standard resulting in an over-valued pound, reduced exports, and a need to cut costs (including wages) by some 10%. Thousands of mill workers were locked out. A government enquiry supported the workers' case. In the General Strike of the following year, the strength of the unions was demonstrated when Bradford's railwaymen, printers and municipal tram workers all came out on strike.

Unemployed camp, Whetley Lane, Manningham, 1906. (Bradford Libraries)

Bradford still exported much of its textiles but world demand was falling, unemployment rose, and wages fell. Between 1928 and 1932 some 400 Bradford textile firms went out of business and Bradford's unemployment rose to a peak in July 1931. The entry of Japan into the textile trade was also bad news. In 1931 the government's depreciation of sterling and the imposition of a 50% import duty on foreign woollen worsted yarn brought about a quick recovery, but there was a lack of investment in new technology and Bradford suffered from the development of rayon and other man-made fibres.

Despite the difficulties experienced by the textile trade during the inter-war years, the worsted textile industry continued to be the largest employer in Bradford and the rise of chain stores such as Marks & Spencer, who bought directly from the factories, and the protectionist policy of the government, saw a partial recovery. New innovations were introduced such as the recovery of grease from wool waste and its sale for use in soap and other oils.

Politics

In politics, Bradford was at the centre of the development of the Labour Party. The bitter strike at Lister's Manningham Mills in 1891 fuelled left-wing socialism. In 1893 the Independent Labour Party was established. Keir Hardie challenged the established parties with his demand for a new party in which working men and women would represent themselves and no longer be dependent on the erratic goodwill of a few reformist Liberals to improve the terrible conditions in which they worked and lived. Wrote Barbara Castle:

> The courage and defiance of the man stirred my blood. I had seen how the wool merchants' daughters at school had looked down on Evelyn Carter [a friend at Bradford Girls' Grammar School], and I could imagine how Hardie felt as he entered the House of Commons in 1892 as the first independent working-class representative, braving the hostility of the top-hatted and frock-coated brigade in his tweed suit and cloth cap, declaring he would be his own man and sit on the Opposition benches whatever government, Liberal or Conservative, was in power.
> (Barbara Castle. *Fighting All the Way*, 1993)

The ILP's declared object was 'to secure the collective ownership of all means of production, distribution and exchange', but it was not a narrow or exclusive sect, it contained middle-class intellectuals as well as militant trade unionists. In 1906 the trade unions joined with the socialist societies like the ILP and the Fabians to form the Labour Party. In Bradford, the ILP kept up the momentum with its socialist Sunday schools, its Labour churches (socialism was merely Christianity in practice), propaganda meetings and the *Bradford Pioneer* newspaper. Bradford had become the political pace-setter of the Labour movement.

Labour regularly became the largest party on Bradford Council, but the Conservatives and the Liberals maintained an Anti-Socialist Alliance to keep them out of power. However, in 1922, two prominent local ILP members, Fred Jowett and William Leach, were returned as MPs for Bradford, and in 1929 Labour won all but one of the four Bradford seats. Fred Jowett had started his working life at the age of eight as a half-timer in a woollen mill. He had been brought up in one of Bradford's notorious back-to-backs with their communal outdoor privy middens serving a whole row without flushing water. In 1892 he became the first Labour man to win a contested seat on the council and was so successful in his campaign to abolish all privy middens that he was made chairman of the Health Committee. He also campaigned for free school meals for undernourished children. In 1924 he was made a Cabinet minister in Ramsay MacDonald's first government.

Another prominent social reformer was Margaret McMillan, pioneer of the nursery school. She came to work for the Bradford ILP and was elected to the Bradford School Board in 1894. Here she managed to get free school meals into some Bradford schools before government legislation gave local authorities the

power to do so in 1906. She continued to campaign for improved child health and instituted medical inspections. At one of the inspections it was found that of the 300 children examined, one hundred had not had their clothes off for six months. As a result, two school baths were opened and the ILP campaigned for more. McMillan championed the value of fresh air and exercise and also focussed on the education of the whole child, learning through play, and starting young. The 1918 Education Act enabled Bradford to open three nursery schools. The McMillan Campus of Bradford College keeps alive the memory of this pioneer.

Open-air school, Thackley, *c.* 1909. (*Report of the School Medical Officer, 1909*, opposite p.76. Courtesy Bradford Libraries)

Housing

The trend of government, national and local, to intervene in social issues continued after the war. The Housing Act of 1919 gave financial encouragement to local councils to provide homes for the working class to rent and of the 23,000 homes built in Bradford between 1919 and 1939 over 10,000 were council houses. Large-scale slum clearance was encouraged by the Housing Act of 1924 and the slums of White Abbey, Wapping and the Broomfields were demolished and their inhabitants re-housed in the new estates at Whetley Lane, Canterbury Avenue, Ravenscliffe, Swain House and Wibsey. After the Second World War further estates were constructed at Buttershaw, Woodside and Allerton, with later development in the 1950s and early '60s at Thorpe Edge, Bierley and Holme Wood. Estates of owner-occupier houses also made their appearance in the planned developments in places such as Heaton, Frizinghall and Wibsey.

Post-war redevelopment, North Wing. (Bradford Libraries)

Building of the Bierley Estate, 1950s. (C.H. Wood. Courtesy Bradford Libraries)

Aerial view of Allerton, one of the new estates. (*Telegraph & Argus*, 19 December 1975. Courtesy Bradford Libraries)

Health

Bradford Council continued to be active in public health. Among the issues tackled were:

- the opening of the Bradford Royal Infirmary in 1936
- the establishment of smokeless zones
- inspection of the town's food markets, abattoirs and bakeries by municipal food inspectors
- the appointment of municipal midwives in 1917, long before other authorities
- the introduction of nursery schools, special schools for handicapped and maladjusted children, and a Bradford School Health Service

The largest enterprise was the provision for an adequate water supply. The introduction of the water closet, domestic washing machines and the greater concern for cleanliness, in addition to an expanding population, created an enormous demand for clean water. In 1904 work started on building Angram and Scar House reservoirs in Nidderdale, thirty miles away. This was a massive engineering project employing some thousand people. Cast-iron and steel conduits originally brought the water thirty-two miles to the Chellow Heights service reservoir and filtration works. A third reservoir, Grimworth, compensated those other districts in the Wharfe Valley whose water was used by Bradford.

Education

Bradford continued its pioneering work in education. The 'Bradford Charter', a proposal by the Education Committee of the Bradford Trades Council in 1916 to raise the school leaving age to sixteen and the provision of universal free compulsory secondary education for all the city's children, was promoted by the ILP. The Education Act of 1918 raised the school leaving age to fourteen and abolished the Victorian 'half-time' system whereby half a child's day was spent in the factory and the other half at school. Priestman, Gregory and Forster schools were opened as central secondary schools, with a curriculum which was more vocationally orientated than previously and by 1928 there was a major restructuring of educational provision along the lines of secondary grammar, selective central and secondary modern schools.

The Act also permitted the establishment of rate-supported nursery schools and two such schools were opened at Princeville and St Anne's (Broomfields) in 1920, with Lilycroft following in 1928. At Lilycroft, the pioneering work of Margaret McMillan was continued by Miriam Lord, who established an international reputation for her work and received an OBE.

Money shortages during the Depression years hampered the work of the Education Committee and there were those who criticised the wisdom of 'over-educating' children, so the demand for schooling on the new post-war housing estates was slow to be met. Only after the 1944 Education Act was the earlier ambitious 'free education for all' policy of the Bradford Trades Council achieved.

Transport

During the First World War, an innovation was made by converting trolleybuses into trolley-lorries carrying goods and parcels to local mills. The early trolleybuses were single-decker, double-deckers being introduced in 1920. Instead of connecting up tram routes as hitherto, direct trolleybus routes from the city centre were introduced with services to Frizinghall along Canal Road and to Bolton Woods. A new service from Town Hall Square to Clayton was opened in 1926 and the Oakenshaw route was extended down the Manchester Road into the city. The success of the 'trackless' led to their replacing tram routes altogether throughout the 1930s, although a couple of tram routes were converted direct to motorbuses.

The closing of tram routes continued during and after the Second World War, but because of the difficulty of obtaining new trolleybuses in this period, these routes were replaced by motorbus services. However, twenty new trolleybuses were delivered between 1949 and 1951 and the Bradford Moor route became trolleybus operated in 1949 and was extended as a through service to Crossflatts. The last tram ran on the Manchester Road route in May 1960.

Horse-drawn transport: provisions cart, Co-op Yard, School Street, Clayton, 1909. (Bradford Libraries)

Cheapside trolleybus turning circle, 1963. (Mrs Bruce. Courtesy Bradford Libraries)

Last day of trams on Church Bank, 23 July 1949. The difficulty trams had on steep hills like Church Bank (cathedral on left) was one reason they gave way to trolley and motorbuses. (Bradford Libraries)

Forster Square from Bolton Road, c. 1959. (Bradford Libraries)

The nationalisation of the electricity industry ended the supply of cheap municipally generated power and cast doubts on the future of the trolleybus service, but the appointment of a new General Manager in 1951 thoroughly revitalised the service. A number of motorbus services were replaced by trolleybuses and the network was extended. Thornbury, Wibsey, Eccleshill, Bierley, Holme Wood and Buttershaw all got a new trolleybus service. In 1961, Bradford celebrated fifty years of trolleybus operation, a year which proved to be the climax of the system's history. There were 193 vehicles, the wiring was well maintained and used modern methods of construction. Turning circles were wide.

Massive redevelopment works in the city centre caused considerable disruption to the trolleybus services and throughout the 1960s routes were closed. By April 1971, Bradford had become the last operator of trolleybuses in Britain and on Friday 24 March 1972 Britain's last public service trolleybus ran its final journey.

Initially, the motorbus supplemented the tram routes and they were run by a mixture of private companies and Bradford Corporation. Competition was fierce, with reliability and safety the casualties, but the Road Traffic Act of 1930 established a system of regulation. Licences were awarded to operators who could guarantee safety and reliability, and routes were agreed by regional Traffic Commissioners. Inevitably, the larger companies began to dominate. Motorbuses proved more successful than the branch railway lines and the trams, and were the most popular form of transport until the rise of the domestic motor car from the 1950s.

While the railways continued to provide fast and regular contact between towns (the introduction of the 'West Riding Limited' in 1937 reduced the journey time to London to three hours five minutes), they were less successful in the hillier areas of Bradford because of the need for gentle gradients. Trolley buses and the motor car were better on the hills and as these new forms of

Chester Street Bus Station, 1954. (Bradford Libraries)

transport developed, some of Bradford's stations closed: Eccleshill, Idle and Thackley in 1931, Esholt in 1940.

Leisure

Increased free time and easier transport saw the development of mass leisure activities. Eleven excursion trains took supporters to London to see Bradford City play Newcastle in the 1911 FA Cup; over 137,000 spectators attended the game and the replay at Old Trafford. Bradford's second soccer team, Bradford Park Avenue, was promoted to the top division in October 1914, and 30,000 people watched them play Bradford City at Valley Parade. The Park Avenue ground in Horton was also a home for Yorkshire Cricket Club and hosted huge crowds for matches against Australia and the traditional Bank Holiday 'Roses' match against Lancashire.

Going to the cinema was by far the most popular public entertainment. Al Jolson's *Singing Fool* was Bradford's first 'talkie', shown at the Savoy Cinema in Darley Street, and by 1939 Bradford had forty-two cinemas. Choir singing, brass bands and amateur dramatics were traditional leisure pursuits that continued. The Civic Playhouse opened in 1929 and in 1931 the Bradford History Pageant took place in Peel Park. This remarkable event, which told the history of Bradford from Roman times to the Industrial Revolution, involved 7,500 schoolchildren in the actual pageant and 16,000 others in displays of drama, music and gymnastics.

The art deco 1930 Sunwin House seen from Kirkgate.

To the Alhambra Theatre, built in 1914, were added purpose-built cinemas such as the New Victoria in Thornton Road in 1930, the Odeon in Manchester Road, and the Ritz in Broadway. The 'art deco' Co-op Emporium (1935) at the corner of Sunbridge Road and Godwin Street survives today. In 1927 warehousing in Bridge Street and Hall Ings was replaced by retail and office accommodation. Surviving examples are Broadway House and Britannia House.

Second World War, 1939-1945

> I returned the other afternoon to my native city of Bradford, where I went to see what damage had resulted from a recent air raid. ... It was astonishing to discover that the familiar large drapers store and the old chapel were no longer there, and that in their place were some blackened ruins with odd pillars and bits of wall still standing ... (J.B. Priestley, *Postscripts*, 1940)

Unlike the previous war, the Second World War came direct to Bradford through the bombing raids of the Luftwaffe. The sulphuric acid works on Canal Road was hit on 30 August 1940 and the following day a hundred people were injured when Lingard's city centre department store was destroyed. Gasmasks were issued, children were evacuated out of the city and air-raid shelters were erected in back gardens. Rationing was introduced for sugar, butter and meat, but other products were in short supply and queuing became commonplace.

The experience learned in the previous war was put to good use as the city mobilised. The British wool supply was brought under the central control of the Wool Control Board with fixed prices and rationing. Despite losing much of their labour force to the war effort, the demand for wool for uniforms was soon fulfilled by the Bradford manufacturers and there was a sufficient surplus to meet the requirements of the civilian population and to maintain a substantial export trade to the USA and the Empire.

1945-1974

Post-war industrial recovery was difficult, particularly in the textile industry. There was a severe shortage of labour and great competition for workers, with salaries greater than the textile trade could offer. The price of raw wool rose rapidly and there was fierce competition from abroad. There was a move to adopt a twenty-four-hour pattern of working in many mills. Some Bradford textile firms bussed in workers from other areas in the region, but the main solution was to employ East European immigrants and, after 1955, Asian workers from India and Pakistan. By 1969, immigrant workers made up more than 10% of the workforce in the woollen and worsted textile industry, mostly from the Indian sub-continent.

Smoky Bradford from Ingleby Road in the 1950s, before smoke control legislation. (Bradford Heritage Recording Unit. Courtesy Bradford Libraries)

Mechanisation in the textile industry. The spinning room at Illingworth & Sons, Thornton Road, 1986. (Bradford Heritage Recording Unit. Courtesy Bradford Libraries)

Perm winding. Date and location unknown. (Bradford Heritage Recording Unit. Courtesy Bradford Libraries)

Even so, the textile industry, Bradford's major employer, was in serious decline, and so, therefore, was the city itself. Innovation, specialisation and the amalgamation of many small family businesses followed. The 1,123 woollen and worsted mills of 1950 shrank to 825 by 1967, and by 1975 a good half of the Bradford industry was in the hands of just fifteen large-scale companies.

New machinery such as the Sulzer loom has reduced the manpower needed to operate the earlier looms; better wool-combing, cleaning and marketing methods have resulted in standardisation; and ring-spinning has replaced the traditional labour-intensive mule-spinning. While this has reduced the labour force, it has provided the economies that have kept Bradford in the textile industry.

Economic Diversity

The contraction in the woollen and worsted trades resulted in the development of other manufacturing trades. Bradford's engineering industry developed from the early metals industry and the present-day Low Moor Alloy Steels continues on its historic site. Together with the electrical and vehicle industries, engineering is a major Bradford employer. In 1891 about a quarter of the metal manufacturing engineering work was in manufacturing textile machinery. Some firms moved into other areas of manufacture, such as Crofts, founded in 1887 (now Renold Chains), who now make transmission equipment in their Thornbury and Dudley Hill sites, and Thomas Wright (Bradford) who now make compressed air machinery.

The range of engineering products is extensive, from tools, trucks and tankers to the precision piston rings made by Hepworth & Grandage (now Federal Mogul Bfd Ltd). This firm began in 1907 as general engineers and employed over 3,000 people in 1969. It played a major role in the war effort, receiving a visit in 1942 from the Prime Minister, Winston Churchill, Minister of Labour

Little now remains of the Low Moor iron works. This is a 30.5-ton rolling mill flywheel from the former Low Moor Steel Works.

Brown, Muff & Co. display
inside the old Foster Square
station, 1930s. (House of
Fraser archives. Courtesy
Bradford Libraries)

Ernest Bevin and the Air Minister. The firm's prosperity was due in large measure to the dramatic increase in the number of motor cars.

Bradford, indeed, once had its own car industry. Benjamin and William Jowett started life as bicycle dealers, going on to motorcycle engines, forming the Jowett Motor Manufacturing Company in 1901, making Jowett cars and the 'Bradford' van. The Jowett Jupiter won its class at the Le Mans twenty-four-hour motor race three years in succession. Motorcycles were the speciality of the Scott Motor Cycle Company, whose founder, Manningham engineer Alfred A. Scott, invented his first twin-cyclinder two-stroke motorcycle in 1909 and Scott motorbikes had numerous successes in the Isle of Man TT races. The company ceased in 1950. Tractors were later manufactured by International Harvesters at their plant at Eccleshill.

Chemical manufacture is a more modern development of Bradford's industrial base. In south Bradford, CIBA (formerly Allied Colloids) produces materials for the textiles, paper and mining industries; A.H. Marks Ltd makes herbicides, largely for export; and BTI. Chemicals produced organic chemicals.

The products manufactured in Bradford are varied. One present-day company (Clearwater Collection) successfully exporting to twenty-three countries makes free-standing baths. A major industry is printing. Fields of Lidget Green was founded in 1850 and is now part of the Reed Group; Lund Humphreys began in Bradford in 1884 and specialised in fine art printing. Other notable firms are Thornton & Pearson, Hallmark, the greeting card giant, and Hart & Clough, recently of Listerhills, now of Cleckheaton.

The changing employments in the city after the war included a rise in the number of staff needed in the commercial sector, particularly in banks, insurance companies and building societies such as the Bradford & Bingley. The expansion of local and central government also created a lively demand for 'white collar' workers.

Mail order is now one of Bradford's largest employers. Its origins can be traced back to the 1830s, when ex-soldier Emilio Fattorini came to Bradford to set up a jewellery business. He sold his wares in local inns on a credit basis and made small regular collections from his clients until the items were paid for. The mail order business began in 1898. A family split occurred in 1912 when Enrico Fattorini left the family business of Empire Stores to start Grattan, which became the largest single company in Europe devoted solely to the mail order trade. In addition to Empire Stores (now Redcats (UK) Plc) and the Gratton Group, a third Bradford company was the Provident Clothing and Supply Company. The massive warehouses of these undertakings cover large areas of western Bradford, straddling Ingleby Road and stretching west to Cemetery Road.

Another success story in the retail trade is that of Morrisons, the supermarket chain. The firm was started in 1899 by William and Hilda Morrison, who sold eggs and butter in Bradford and Dewsbury markets. Son Ken took over his parents' firm and in 2004 the company had 550 supermarkets.

In the field of electrical engineering, the English Electric Company (formerly the Phoenix Dynamo Manufacturing Company) began in Thornbury in 1918. The firm produced dynamos, generators, gears and electric motors. It has now been absorbed by other companies. Thorne Electrical, situated in the Lidget Green area, began life as Bairds, using a former 1893 textile mill. Its main product was television sets and in 1974 it employed 4,500 people producing 40% of all colour television sets in the UK. It closed shortly afterwards.

Filtronic Components and Pace Micro Technology are just down the road in Saltaire. Filtronic plc is an aggregate of several companies whose activities cover designing and making equipment for mobile telephone base stations, electronic defence systems for military aircraft and warships, communication boxes for cable companies, and making filters and antennae for mobile phones. Filtronic has grown in twenty years to become a multi-national company manufacturing digital television set-top boxes and electronic equipment for overseas electronics companies.

Many of these newer industries are located away from the traditional valley bottoms to be nearer the ring roads. With the coming of the trans-Pennine M62 and its easy links to the national motorway network, there has been a growth of 'trading estates' such as the Euroway estate by the M606 motorway spur into Bradford and the nearby land vacated by the iron mining industry in the Oakenshaw area.

A 2004 survey by Parcelforce Worldwide revealed that Bradford exported more goods than anywhere else in Yorkshire and Humberside. Clearly, Bradford's long tradition of trading across the world, especially from its days as the worsted capital of the world, has continued. Maybe its multi-national population gives it more of an outward-looking focus.

In 1979, a Tourism Officer was appointed by the council, and, despite initial scepticism, tourism is now one of Bradford's biggest industries.

Transport

The competition from the car caused a decline in the use of railways, which had also been run down during the war years. Stations on the Queensbury line and others south of Bradford were closed in the 1950s. It was in the context of increasing losses on rail services as car ownership increased that Dr Beeching produced his report, *The Re-Shaping of British Railways*, in 1963. Beeching saw no future for local rail services and recommended widescale closures. Further lstation closures in Bradford included Laisterdyke, Manningham, Frizinghall, Laisterdyke and Low Moor. In recent years there has been a mild revival in the rail system, with direct express services to London resumed, electrification on the Airedale and Wharfedale lines, new rolling stock, and new stations at Frizinghall, Saltaire and Crossflatts.

One of the many disused rail bridges in Bradford. Hammerton Lane.

The *Yorkshire Pullman* leaving Forster Square station, 30 May 1967. (Bradford Libraries)

In 1974 the West Yorkshire Passenger Transport Executive was born to provide the public transport services that were formerly run by the local authorities and which were integrated with local rail services.

In 1930, Leeds and Bradford councils purchased land on high ground at Yeadon and built a small aerodrome which was completed in 1939. It was requisitioned by the Air Ministry for defence purposes and some 4,500 aircraft were built there. It was returned to the councils in 1959, when freight and passenger services commenced. The Leeds/Bradford airport is a popular departure point for business and holiday flights with a wide regional catchment area. Some 2.7 million passengers were expected in 2005.

The ever-growing domination by the motor car is demonstrated in the massive road-building programmes: the M606 opened in 1975 linking Bradford to the East-West M62 and then with the M1 to London, the Euroway Trading Estate is adjacent, the Shipley-Airedale Road was built to take traffic out of the city centre, the thirty-year saga of the Aire Valley trunk road rumbles on, and the ring roads are congested.

City Reconstruction

After the Second World War, the physical reconstruction of the city was started in earnest. The post-war planning theories of zoning areas of a city for specific purposes, of sweeping away Victorian clutter and accommodating the motor car, found an energetic proponent in the appointment of S.G. Wardley as City Engineer and Surveyor in 1946:

> There were minor murmurs of protest at the removal of Peel Square and the Kassapian warehouse (1957) and outrage on the part of one or two building connoisseurs at the demolition of the Court House in Hall Ings a year later in 1958, for the benefit of a car park. Forster Square was ruined as a proper attractive open public space, Tyrrell Street and Collinson's Café were swept away completely to be replaced by chain store developments such as C & A and Arndale, whose standardised high-rise designs were indistinguishable from any other city. Outraged public opinion finally found its voice when Swan Arcade in Market Street was proposed for demolition in 1962. The protests of the Victorian Society were publicly backed by J.B. Priestley and the artist David Hockney, but to no avail. The building was no more by 1963. (Gary Firth, *A History of Bradford*)

In 1966, a building was opened on derelict land in the Listerhills area for the Bradford College of Advanced Technology, which had pioneering departments in textile and chemical technology, mechanical, civil, electrical and chemical engineering, as well as mathematics and physics. It achieved university status that same year, its first chancellor being the Prime Minister, Harold Wilson. In the same period, the Westbrook extension to Bradford's Technical College was built alongside the original (1882) Technical School building, and in 1967 the new eight-storey central library opened in Prince's Way, the biggest municipal library in Europe at the time. It included a Library Theatre used by numerous local societies until sold to the National Museum of Photography, Film and Television for its Cinerama and other film presentations.

1974 saw the completion of a second stage of the city centre redevelopment with the new Magistrates' Courts, Police Headquarters, a transport interchange, the Norfolk Gardens Hotel (now the Hilton) and several large office blocks, including the headquarters of the Provincial Building Society and Wardley House (which contained a theatre that remained empty until occupied by the National Museum of Photography, Film and Television). These buildings replaced Town Hall Square, Exchange Station (the railhead was taken back to the southern side of Bridge Street and incorporated into the massive Transport Interchange) and the Majestic Hotel at the bottom of Manchester Road.

Bradford – concrete and glass style. Jacob's Well.

Provincial House; another brave 1960s Bradford building now demolished.

Metropolitan Bradford

> In the thirteenth century, the de Lacys made an administrative decision to give
> market and administrative status to the tiny rural settlement of Bradford. By
> so doing they established centralising forces which resulted eventually in the
> incorporation of the cluster of villages and hamlets of Bradford Dale into an
> integrated commercial and administrative community – a town. (C. Richardson, *A
> Geography of Bradford*)

Commerce and administration continued to grow and during the last two
centuries acquired a regional importance which has quite outgrown the earlier
valley community. The 1972 Local Government Act represented another
decision, this time by central government, which once more changed the nature
of 'Bradford'. On 1 April 1974, the Bradford Metropolitan District Council
came into being with ninety-three councillors (Conservatives fifty-three, Labour
thirty-one, Liberal nine). The council was formed by joining the city with the
neighbouring councils in Airedale and Wharfedale. The new Metropolitan
District had a population of 462,000 in an area of 91,500 acres. The population
is now (mid-2003 estimate) 467,665.

To celebrate one hundred years of city status in 1997, the area in front of
the City Hall was redeveloped as a large traffic-free public space, Centenary
Square. The tall office-block buildings known as Provincial House opposite the
City Hall were demolished and replaced by a more 'human'-sized city centre
café and bar development. The much derided glass and aluminium office
blocks of Midland House and Forster House and the unpopular subways are
being demolished in the 'Connecting the City' project to better link the central
shopping area with Little Germany and the cathedral. Buildings on Bridge Street
have been redeveloped for residential apartments in an effort to bring back the
city centre living that has been so successful in other cities. The 'Gateways'

Suburban Bradford. Bolton
Woods.

Landscaped suburb. Idle.

project is improving access to the city in the Leeds Road area, while the Forster Square Development is sweeping away the cramped Cheapside area to provide a more open area with public spaces, shops and more parking. Forster Square railway station has already been redesigned and a large and busy retail park built on the site of the old railway sidings. Further plans are afoot to develop the western side of the city centre.

One of the Bradford icons is Lister's Mill chimney. Lister's Mill, the Grade II-listed building dating back to 1871, had fallen into disuse and decay as the textile industry died – a derelict and depressing reminder of Bradford's once-great textile heritage. But the building is now being redeveloped for both residential apartments and retail and work space.

One Landscape – Many Views: Bradfordians Today

Bradford is a cosmopolitan city; it has been host to thousands of migrants for two centuries, longer even. In 1971 one in ten of its population was born outside the United Kingdom and it had a third of the immigrant population of West Yorkshire.

In the nineteenth century, the German and Irish immigrations were the most noticeable, and both have left their mark. At the beginning of the twentieth century there was an influx of Italians, most of whom settled initially in the 'Poets Quarter' off the Otley Road to the north-east of the city centre.

The Second World War brought an influx of ex-soldiers, refugees and émigré communities from the territories occupied by the Soviet Union: Poland, the Ukraine, Lithuania, Latvia and Estonia, plus many from Hungary and Yugoslavia. These peoples, too, brought their own culture and traditions.

The short-lived Forster House. Built 1972, demolished 2004.

Change, ever change! The 1960s Forster House being demolished in 2004. The old façade of Forster Square station, now left standing by its trains (which were re-located further out of town a decade earlier), survive still – just.

left A 1987 street scene. Bridge Street, outside the Transport
Interchange. (Bradford Heritage Recording Unit. Courtesy Bradford
Libraries)

below Wakefield Road Sikh Temple. (*Telegraph & Argus*, 23 March
1976. Courtesy Bradford Libraries)

above Sport brings together
many peoples.

right Ethnic enterprise in an
old Laisterdyke.

Other immigrants followed, of which the largest groups were those from the West Indies, India, Pakistan, Bangladesh and East Africa.

Bradford has often been in the national spotlight on race and ethnic issues, often for the wrong reasons, but as a place where a large number of people from different ethnic and cultural backgrounds co-exist, the attention is now more positive. Problems now tend to be the more general ones of society as a whole, such as employment, crime and housing. New social groupings and affiliations develop. The election of Mohammad Ajeeb as the UK's first Asian Lord Mayor in 1985 and of Marsha Singh as a Bradford MP in 1997, were signs of an increasingly integrated community.

Events, too, bind people. On 26 May 1976, Bradfordians rejoiced when Richard Dunn, a Bradford scaffolder, fought five rounds with Mohammed Ali for the World Heavyweight Boxing Championship and marked his achievement by naming the Richard Dunn Sports Centre after him when it opened at Odsal in May 1978. Between April 1977 and January 1981, Bradford and surrounding areas in West Yorkshire were terrorised by the Yorkshire Ripper, who murdered thirteen women. We shared the unwelcome fear this brought. On 11 May 1985, fifty-six people died in a fire at the ground of Bradford City Football Club during a match celebrating the winning of the Third Division; this brought us together. We collectively grieved and nearly £4.5 million was raised for the Bradford City Disaster Fund. We rejoiced in 1986 when Joe Johnson beat Steve Davis to become Snooker's World Champion. We rejoiced in 1999 when Bradford City gained promotion to the Premier League, and collectively groaned when they were relegated two years later. We were proud when Bradford was designated Britain's 'Curry Capital' in 1991!

The diversity that multiculturalism brings to Bradford makes it an exciting place. Whatever our origins, we all share the same space.

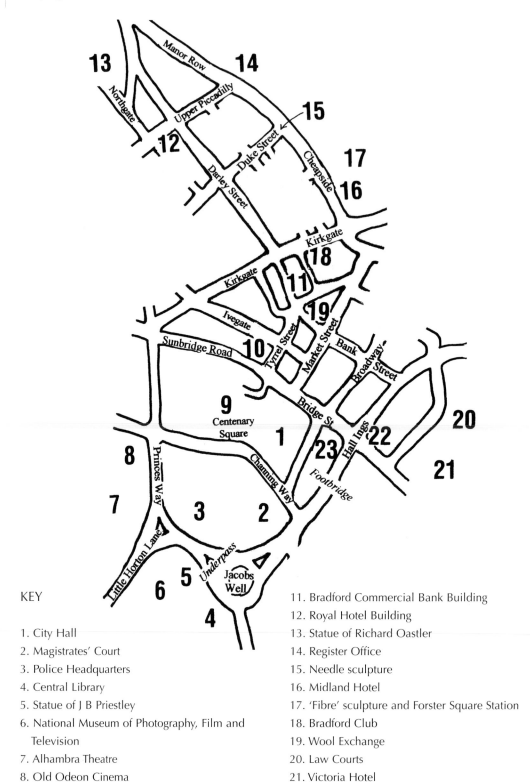

KEY

1. City Hall
2. Magistrates' Court
3. Police Headquarters
4. Central Library
5. Statue of J B Priestley
6. National Museum of Photography, Film and
   Television
7. Alhambra Theatre
8. Old Odeon Cinema
9. Valley Parade Fire Memorial
10. Prudential Assurance Building

11. Bradford Commercial Bank Building
12. Royal Hotel Building
13. Statue of Richard Oastler
14. Register Office
15. Needle sculpture
16. Midland Hotel
17. 'Fibre' sculpture and Forster Square Station
18. Bradford Club
19. Wool Exchange
20. Law Courts
21. Victoria Hotel
22. St. George's Hall
23. Bradford-on-Sea

A Walk in the City

The obvious place to start a walk in Bradford is outside the front of the magnificent City Hall in Centenary Square. Here are to be found those two essentials for the visitor, the Tourist Information Office, and toilets!

The City Hall was opened in 1873 as a building fit for the expanding and prosperous town that Bradford had become. Built of locally quarried stone, it was designed by local architects Lockwood & Mawson. The Campanile (clock tower) is based upon the one in Florence, the Palazzo Vecchio; it stands 220 feet high and has a two-octave thirteen-bell carillon. Look above the main entrance at the statues of Queen Elizabeth and Queen Victoria, then seek out the thirty-two other monarchs (and republican Oliver Cromwell) placed in the niches between the windows at the second-storey level!

Turn right, if you are facing the entrance, and cross over the road, Channing Way, to the lake (and fountain if you are in luck).

To the left is the magistrates' and coroner's court building, built in a tasteful modern style with vertical panels and opened by the Queen in 1974. To its right is the striking Police HQ with its glass-clad walls, and opened at the same time.

Make for the gap between the two and, keeping the Magistrates' Courts to your left, go into the subway ahead. For those who dislike subways, have no fear, almost immediately you will find yourself in an open-air shrub-filled amphitheatre.

The subway has murals painted on its wall depicting films based in Bradford, such as *The Dresser*, *Billy Liar* and *The Railway Children*, and some local buildings.

Taking the right-hand fork and going up the steps on your left you will find yourself outside the Central Library.

left City Hall.

below Magistrates' Court
(right) and Police Headquarters
(left).

Central Library.

City Hall from the Library.

The eight-floor Central Library was the first city-centre library building to be built in Europe after the Second World War. It was opened in 1967 and was designed along the then fashionable subject department principal where reference and lending books were shelved together in specialist departments. There is an excellent view of the City Hall and other buildings in the city centre from outside the library; even better if you go inside to the fifth floor Local Studies department! Admission is free.

Turning north (left with your back to the library) walk round the Pictureville Cinema (once the Library Theatre) which has the UK's only public cinerama screen. Round the corner you will see a statue of J.B. Priestley.

J.B. Priestley (1894-1984), playwright, novelist and journalist, was born in Bradford. Read the inscription on the statute and guess what the Grand Old Man is thinking about as he looks over the city of his birth! Behind Priestley is the National Museum of Photography, Film and Television. The NMPFTV is a major visitor attraction in the north of England. In addition to the exhibits relating to the visual media the world over, there is a huge IMAX screen which gives daily film shows. Admission to the museum is free and there is an excellent café.

Statue of J.B. Priestley outside the National Museum of Photography, Film and Television.

Continue across Little Horton Lane, past the war memorial and the statue of Queen Victoria and her two lions behind it, to the Alhambra Theatre ahead.

The Alhambra Theatre, opened in 1914, and extensively refurbished in 1986, is a jewel in the City's crown. Its domes and upper area were originally painted red. It is Bradford's main theatre offering everything from ballet to pantomime. Beyond the Alhambra is the Odeon Cinema. Called the New Victoria when it was built in 1930, it was, prior to its 1970s modernisation, the largest cinema in the north of England. It is empty now, alas, and facing possible demolition.

National Museum of Photography, Film and Television.

Continue past the Odeon and cross over the road to your right at the traffic lights, back towards the City Hall, and walk to the centre of Centenary Square.

On your right is the Police HQ building and to the left is the new café area. Near the middle of Centenary Square is a memorial to those who lost their lives in the Bradford Fire Disaster of 1986 when fifty-six people died while watching a football match. The sculpture was presented by the citizens of Hamm in Germany, one of Bradford's twin towns. From here there is a fine view of late Victorian and Edwardian buildings to the left of the City Hall. Look out for the ornate dark red-brick Prudential Assurance Building (a rare example of a building not built of local stone), the green dome of Britannia House, and St George's Hall to the right.

Memorial to Queen Victoria.

right The Alhambra Theatre.

below The Odeon Cinema (disused).

The Police Headquarters.

The Centenary Square Bistro.

above The Valley Parade Fire Memorial.

right Rimmington's on Bridge Street.

below Britannia House.

Cross the road near to the Prudential Building. You are crossing the site of the   Prudential Assurance Building.
Sun Bridge, one of the earliest crossings of the Bradford Beck. (The Beck is
fully built over and can, alas, no longer be seen in the city centre.) Continue
straight ahead on the pedestrianised Tyrrel Street.

Ivegate and Queensgate are two narrow streets, now pedestrianised, going up
to your left. They are reminders of the old Bradford with its jostling crowds
and lively shops. A green plaque on the Lloyds Bank building in Ivegate
commemorates the birth here of John Sharp (1644-1713), who became
Archbishop of York, and the stay of General Thomas Fairfax during the Civil
War.

Ahead of you at the next junction is one of the finest commercial buildings in
the city. The Bradford Commercial Bank (now Nat West) is a particularly fine
mock Gothic building from an age when banks vied with each other to have
the grandest buildings. It has a corner turret of ornate stonework. A peek inside
gives a glimpse of a breathtakingly decorated ceiling. On your right you will
see the Wool Exchange which we will come to later.

Go up Bank Street to your left, continue across Kirkgate with its mixture of old
and new buildings, and carry on up the pedestrianised Darley Street, one the

Tyrrel Street.

Bradford Commercial
Bank building.

main shopping streets of Bradford. Keep going for another block of tall, grand buildings beyond the pedestrianised area till you reach the crossroads at the top.

This is Rawson Square, and around here are some particularly fine Victorian buildings. You will probably be standing beneath the former Royal Hotel, the name is embossed in stone several stories up! Through the square to the left you will see the rather brutish modern tower block of the Yorkshire Building Society, and silhouetted is the rather spindly Rawson Hotel. The equally splendid, but better preserved, Masonic Hall is across the road. A little to the left of Rawson Square and across the road into Northgate is the statute of Richard Oastler comforting two children. Oastler was a social reformer who championed the reduction of the long hours which children had to work in the early part of the nineteenth century.

Royal Hotel building.

Returning to Rawson Square, take Upper Piccadilly to the east, downhill, to join Manor Row.

On the other side of Manor Row is the fine building which now houses the Register Office, recognisable by the royal coats of arms above the entrance. Designed by architects Andrews & Pepper, it has a quiet, well-proportioned, tasteful façade. Although built in 1877, the style is more Georgian than the extravagant municipal Gothic that characterises many buildings in the area. It once housed the office of the Poor Law Guardians. Walk down the hill and admire the massive buildings that were once warehouses and are now being renovated as offices and nightclubs. This was once the heart of the textile area and the hoists can still been seen on some of the buildings. One block down on the right, you will see The Needle, a sculpture commemorating Bradford's textile heritage.

Statue of Richard Oastler.

The Midland Hotel is at the bottom of the hill on the left, by the entrance to Forster Square railway station, to which the hotel owed its presence. Like banks and town halls, the railway companies vied with each other the have the biggest and the best. The actor Sir Henry Irving died here in 1905.

Take a look at the roadway to the hotel's left that goes down to the station and you will see the route taken by the many horse-drawn bale-laden wagons of cloth down to the rail head. A retail park now covers the rail sidings and the station was 'downsized' in the 1980s, with a massive tax office built on the old station site. However, a plaque in the present booking offices commemorates Britain's first Pullman service which left for London St Pancras on 1 June 1874. Admire Ian Randall's sculpture, 'Fibre', and ground patterning in St Blaise Square here, celebrating many varieties of communication.

At the time of writing, the Forster Square area was being redeveloped, but look across from the Midland hotel to the elegant Post Office building (no longer a post office) and the cathedral behind it. Across the road from the Midland Hotel go up Kirkgate for a few yards and turn second left into narrow Piece Hall Yard.

The Needle.

above Kirkgate.

right The Register Office.

The Midland Hotel.

On the left of Piece Hall Yard is The Bradford Club. Built in 1865 in Victorian Gothic style, this elegant ladies' and gentlemen's club has one of Bradford's finest interiors (viewing by appointment only). Opened as a lunch club for the business community, it is a popular venue for functions. Further down on the right is the Peace Museum, which has displays on peace education and banners, posters and paintings of peace campaigns. It celebrates Bradford's long association with the peace movement.

At the bottom of Piece Hall Yard is the new glass-front of Waterstone's bookshop, situated in the Wool Exchange. Go left to the main entrance of the Wool Exchange under the clock tower.

The Wool Exchange is magnificently unmistakable. This gloriously Gothic building was opened in 1867 and is another building designed by Lockwood & Mawson. The building boasts a fine 150-foot high clock tower. At the clock tower entrance stand the statues of Saint Blaise, the patron saint of wool workers, holding the traditional form of wool comb, and on his right is King Edward III, who did much for the wool trade. On two of the outside walls of the Wool Exchange are the sculptured heads of famous people in British history. Starting at the main entrance and going clockwise they are: Richard Cobden, Titus Salt, Robert Stephenson, James Watt, Richard Arkwright, Samuel Cunliffe Lister, William Gladstone, Lord Palmerston, James Cook, Admiral Anson, Sir Walter Raleigh, Sir Francis Drake and Christopher Columbus.

Inside the Wool Exchange is a stunning hammer-beam roof with flying angels carrying the shields of the most important towns and cities of Yorkshire. The statue of Richard Cobden, who championed free trade and was the hero of the wool traders who used to meet and haggle here, stands here still. The Wool Exchange is now a bookshop, but the Victorian interior decoration of marble pillars, coloured tiling, arches and window tracery has been retained, and the smell of coffee and new books assaults the senses! A good place to break your tour.

Past the Wool Exchange you enter Bank Street. Turn left, cross over Market Street and also the shopping street of Broadway, and you will see ahead, across the main road, the startling black-glazed building opened in 1981 housing the printing presses of the local newspaper, the *Telegraph & Argus*. At the time of writing, a huge poster proclaiming 'One Landscape – Many Views' covers most of its side. To its right is the 1853 Milligan warehouse building that now houses the newspaper offices

The *Telegraph & Argus* Print Room.

Cross over the road (Hall Ings), go left a few yards, and at the entrance of Drake Street opposite go up the steps to the left to the building above that you can just see.

Before turning right to walk to the front of the building, the Law Courts, look left for the seats by which you can look at the panorama of the eastern end of the city. The historic Eastbrook Hall, built in 1903 as a Methodist meeting place, can be seen on the left of the Leeds Road to your right, while ahead is Little Germany, the mercantile centre established by German immigrants in the mid-nineteenth century. The quality of the architecture – most of the buildings have listed status – is impressive, and Little Germany is well worth a stroll if you have time. If you look carefully you can just see the pinnacles of Bradford Cathedral peeping over the warehouses.

The Law Courts are on the site of the old Exchange Station and opened in 1998. In the space in front of the Crown Courts is a striking sculpture of a butterfly, a tribute to the Bradford-born composer Frederick Delius, and across the way is Bradford's other major railway hotel. Looking like a large French chateau is the Victoria Hotel (though neither hotel is now owned by any rail company). Like the Midland, the Victoria can boast many famous guests.

Continue past the right-hand side of the Victoria Hotel to Bridge Street, cross over, and walk down to the bottom.

above The Law Courts.

opposite above Rogerson Building, Little Germany.

opposite below The Victoria Hotel.

Across the road to your right you will see the richly carved façade of St George's   St George's Hall.
Hall, Bradford's major concert hall. Built in 1853 to a design by Lockwood &
Mawson, the neo-classical façade marks it out from other buildings. Rather
unusually, it is built of Leeds stone which looks and weathers differently from
Bradford stone.

For a final panorama, turn left at the traffic lights, pass in front of the Hilton
Hotel, and cross the dual carriageway by the bridge you will see in front of you.

From this bridge you will recognize many of the buildings already visited: the
Central Library and the Magistrates' Courts up the hill, the City Hall in front,
and to the right there is a good view of St George's Hall and the massive bulk
of the 1929 Britannia House to its left. Bradford's Hilton Hotel is to the right.
Back along the bridge is the way to the Transport Interchange, with its bus and
rail connections.

Continue over the bridge and descend.

Keeping the City Hall to your right, you will be back in Centenary Square.

The 1905 City Hall extension.

Looking up Hall Ings from the footbridge to the Central Library and Wardley House (right).

Looking down Hall Ings towards Britannia House (left) and St George's Hall (right).

Further Reading

There are a large number of books and other resources available on the history of Bradford – far too many to list here. For further information on these try the local history shelves in the local libraries, the bibliographies in the books listed below, or the website of the Bradford Historical and Antiquarian Society (www. bradfordhistorical.fsnet.co.uk). The following are some of the titles in print at the time of writing (June 2005):

Birdsall, M., Szekely, G. and Walker, P., *The Illustrated History of Bradford's Suburbs*, Breedon Books, 2002.

Duckett, Bob, *Aspects of Bradford: Discovering Local History*, Wharncliffe Publishing, 1999.

Duckett, Bob, *Aspects of Bradford 2: Discovering Local History*, Wharncliffe Publishing, 2000.

Firth, Gary, *A History of Bradford*, Phillimore, 1997.

Greenhalf, Jim, *It's a Mean Old Scene: A History of Modern Bradford from 1974*, Redbeck Press, 2003.

Leslie, Michael, *Bradford City Hall: A History and Guide*, City of Bradford MDC, 1997.

Lister, Derek A.J., *Bradford's Own*. Sutton Publishing, 2004.

Lockwood, Stephen, *Bradford Trolleybuses*, Middleton Press, 2003.

Rank, Carol, ed. *City of Peace: Bradford's Story*, Bradford Libraries, 1997.

Richardson, C., *The Bradford Region: Studies in its Human Geography*, Bradford Libraries, Archives and Information Service, 2002.

Singh, Ramindar, *The Struggle for Racial Justice*, The Author, 2002.

Other resources of a general nature are:

The Bradford Antiquary: The Journal of the Bradford Historical and Antiquarian Society, 1878 to date. Annual.

City of Bradford Metropolitan District Council *Bradford in the Twentieth Century: guide to resources and select reading list*. Compiled by Sarah Powell. Available from the Local Studies Library, Central Library, Princes Way, Bradford BD1 1NN.

Now out of print but particularly useful are:

Fieldhouse, J. *Bradford*, Longman, 1972. Revised edition published by Watmoughs and Bradford Libraries, 1978.

Hird, Horace, *How a City Grows: Historical Notes on the City of Bradford*, The Author, 1966.

Hird, Horace, *Bradford in History: Twenty-four Essays on Life by the Broad Ford from the Celtic Age to the Present Day*, The Author, 1968.

James, David, *Bradford*, Ryburn Publishing, 1990.

Johnson, Edward Hotspur, *The Bradford Almanack*, Bradford Libraries, 1990.

Richardson, C., *A Geography of Bradford*, University of Bradford, 1976.

Scruton, William, *Pen and Pencil Pictures of Old Bradford*, Thomas Brear, 1889.

Sheeran, George, *The Victorian Houses of Bradford*, Bradford Libraries, 1990.

Contacts

The Local Studies Service, Central Library, Prince's Way, Bradford BD1 1NN
Tel. 01274 433661; Fax 01274 433660; Email: local.studies@bradford.gov.uk

Bradford Industrial Museum, Moorside Mills, Moorside Road, Eccleshill, Bradford BD2 3HP
Tel. 01274 435900; Fax 01274 636362

Bolling Hall Museum, Bowling Hall Road, Bradford BD4 7LP
Tel. 01274 723057; Fax 01274 726220

West Yorkshire Archive Service, Bradford Office, 15 Canal Road, Bradford BD1 4AT
Tel. 01274 731931; Fax 01274 734013; Email: bradford@wyjs.org.uk

University of Bradford Library Special Collections, J.B.Priestley Library, University of Bradford, Bradford BD7 1DP
Tel. 01274 235256; Email: special-collections@bradford.ac.uk

Index

Illustrations are included. (Col. 1 = number 1 in the colour section)